CMMI for Development

Implementation Guide

Mukund Chaudhary
Abhishek Chopra

Apress®

CMMI for Development: Implementation Guide

Mukund Chaudhary
Noida, Uttar Pradesh, India

Abhishek Chopra
Faridabad, Haryana, India

ISBN-13 (pbk): 978-1-4842-2528-8
DOI 10.1007/978-1-4842-2529-5

ISBN-13 (electronic): 978-1-4842-2529-5

Library of Congress Control Number: 2016961816

Managing Director: Welmoed Spahr
Lead Editor: Nikhil Karkal
Editorial Board: Steve Anglin, Pramila Balan, Laura Berendson, Aaron Black, Louise Corrigan, Jonathan Gennick, Robert Hutchinson, Celestin Suresh John, Nikhil Karkal, James Markham, Susan McDermott, Matthew Moodie, Natalie Pao, Gwenan Spearing
Coordinating Editor: Prachi Mehta
Copy Editor: Patrick Meader
Compositor: SPi Global
Indexer: SPi Global

Distributed to the book trade worldwide by Springer Science+Business Media New York, 233 Spring Street, 6th Floor, New York, NY 10013. Phone 1-800-SPRINGER, fax (201) 348-4505, e-mail orders-ny@springer-sbm.com, or visit www.springeronline.com. Apress Media, LLC is a California LLC and the sole member (owner) is Springer Science + Business Media Finance Inc (SSBM Finance Inc). SSBM Finance Inc is a **Delaware** corporation.

For information on translations, please e-mail rights@apress.com, or visit www.apress.com.

Apress and friends of ED books may be purchased in bulk for academic, corporate, or promotional use. eBook versions and licenses are also available for most titles. For more information, reference our Special Bulk Sales–eBook Licensing web page at www.apress.com/bulk-sales.

Any source code or other supplementary materials referenced by the author in this text are available to readers at www.apress.com. For detailed information about how to locate your book's source code, go to www.apress.com/source-code/. Readers can also access source code at SpringerLink in the Supplementary Material section for each chapter.

Printed on acid-free paper

We would like to dedicate this book to all professionals who believe in Quality and Process Improvement.

Contents at a Glance

Contents

About the Authors

Mukund Chaudhary has been working in the IT industry for almost a decade; most of that experience has been in managing software projects. He is enamored of technology and keeps himself up-to-date through avid reading. In his leisure time, he can be found reading articles on current affairs and technologies alike. He has coauthored three books, and he believes that learning never stops, as long as a person is alive. He lives in Noida/NCR, India, in a joint family with his wife, Nandita, and son, Madhav. He is @mukund002 on Twitter.

Abhishek Chopra is a Quality Manager by profession and an adventurer by nature. He is passionate about quality, and he has worked with various MNCs to implement CMMI.

He loves to talk about process improvements for hours and hours, and he does not care whether this bores the other person! In this book, he has put his key focus on sharing his experiences, with the aim of helping readers in implementing the CMMI in a simple manner. He lives in Delhi/NCR, India with his mother, Anita, and wife, Rhythm. He is @AB_55 on Twitter.

Acknowledgments

I would like to thank my organization, which gave me the chance to understand the concept of CMMI and supported me with my training needs. I'd also like to express my gratitude to everyone who has supported me at all times. I am also thankful to the editors for their inspiring guidance and their friendly advice, especially Nikhil Karkal.

I would also like to thank all the colleagues and friends who have helped me. I sincerely thank everyone, including my parents, my wife, friends, and teammates who encouraged me while writing. Special thanks to my grandfather, the late Kameshwar Chaudhary, who always inspired me to write.

—Mukund Chaudhary

I would like to thank my elder sister, Meenakshi, who guided my career to become a quality professional and introduced me to the concept of CMMI and its importance in software development. My sister and brother-in-law, Raj Stanley, have always been greatly supportive of me, and I will always be thankful to them. I am also thankful to the editors and Apress team for their inspiring guidance and friendly advice, especially Nikhil Karkal.

I would also like to thank my colleagues and friends, Mukund and Anushka, who encouraged me to write and share my experiences. Special thanks to my mother, who is always an inspiration to me.

—Abhishek Chopra

CHAPTER 1

■ ■ ■

CMMI Overview

Many companies want to improve their processes, but they don't know which process model to follow to make head way in process implementation. This is a real point of confusion for many in the IT industry, as these process models are seen as a hindrance to working efficiently, and too much process documentation might affect their productivity. Also, in today's fast-paced world, customers put a lot of pressure on their contractors to deliver faster, but they don't want this fast delivery to compromise the quality of the work.

So the question arises, "How can you guarantee your software product's quality (whether it is a web site or any other software product/application)?" This becomes more complex when you have a large development team; and moreover, when you have teams which are distributed in different parts of the world or different cities in the same country. Without a defined process, communication with distributed teams can become complex.

Now, you might be wondering how CMMI is going to help? CMMI is very vast, and every practice mentioned in the model may not work for everyone, which may seem impractical to many during the first attempt at using it.

But we are jumping the gun a bit. What we really need to focus on initially is how we can mold CMMI to deliver the process and product results we require.

We need to ask ourselves a few questions here: What we are trying to improve? Is it a process, a product, or a team? Is it revenue, which is important for the company's existence in the longer run? Implementing CMMI is an investment of time and money, but this investment will certainly provide ROI to the company in a positive way.

And again, there are more questions: Who are the first people in your organization who will think or analyze whether CMMI is important for them and the organization? And how will these people implement CMMI step-by-step, so that the organization can head forward in the CMMI way?

Well, your senior-management professionals in the organization have to jump in and understand the real value of CMMI best practices before they force or tell the delivery teams to become process oriented in everything they do.

You might wonder here, "Why senior management?" Well, why not? They are the people who make most of the decisions in the organization, mostly for the good of the organization. It is their job to make it is easier for the delivery team to produce the required products and results.

The top-down approach works well the most organizations. If senior management agrees to something, it can assure that a directive is followed by everyone else. Otherwise, teams which are at the lower level will feel reluctant in following the process-oriented approach because they will see it as an overhead, which is the wrong notion.

And why it is a wrong notion? Because every step or action we take in our project or product development is a process itself, though we don't always realize this. For example, writing the code for a module and conducting unit tests are also part of a process.

CMMI talks about all the different process areas which a process-oriented organization should define and follow. What are all these process areas? In this book, we'll walk you through these different process areas, to give you a better understanding of CMMI.

© Mukund Chaudhary 2017

M. Chaudhary and A. Chopra, *CMMI for Development*, DOI 10.1007/978-1-4842-2529-5_1

In this chapter, we will provide an overview of CMMI, describe its evolution, and then cover where it can be used and by whom.

Before moving to CMMI, let's cover what a process is. A *process* can be defined as a set of inter-related activities which take some input, and then generate output with a given purpose. Generally, a process involves tools and methods.

Put more simply, you can define process as a series of actions or steps taken to achieve a particular goal. A typical process is:

- Simple

- Well documented

- Measurable

- Flexible

- Stable

Process is important because the quality of the product depends a lot on the quality of the processes that we use to create it. It is for this reason that CMMI has been developed with

Hence, the quality of the process is very crucial to the quality of the end product. CMMI has been developed with a strong emphasis on the relationship between process and product quality.

1.1 What Is CMMI?

CMMI is about collecting the characteristics of effective processes, and then using this information to provide guidance for improving an organization's processes. The end goal is to make it easier for an organization to develop products or solutions by improving its ability to manage the development, acquisition, and maintenance of its products or services.

CMMI is a model; it tells us what to do, but not how to do it. It is not a set of practices and methodology but it is the concept that we need to apply to the organization to get mature from a process perspective.

> *The Capability Maturity Model Integration (CMMI) is a capability improvement model that can be adapted to solve any performance issue at any level of the organization in any industry. The Model provides guidelines and recommendations for helping your organization diagnose problems and improve performance. Used by over 5000 organizations in more than 70 countries all over the world, CMMI helps you identify and achieve measurable business goals.*

> — CMMI Institute

1.1.1 A CMMI Overview

CMMI was developed by a group of expert professionals from industry, government, and the Software Engineering Institute (SEI) at CMU. A CMMI model is set of guidance, and it can be used as a framework for appraising the process maturity of an organization. CMMI currently addresses three important area of interest:

- Product and service development—CMMI for Development (CMMI-DEV)

- Service establishment, management—CMMI for Services (CMMI-SVC)

- Product and service acquisition—CMMI for Acquisition (CMMI-ACQ).

The first two areas of interest are widely used and in high demand. In this book, we will be covering the first area, product and service development, which is also popularly known as CMMI-DEV.

CMMI-DEV v1.3 is a reference model that covers activities for developing both products and services. These days, many organizations from various industries (e.g., software, defense, aerospace, banking, automobile, manufacturing, and telecommunications) implement and follow CMMI-DEV v1.3 industry best practices.

CMMI-DEV contains practices for process areas (i.e., project management, process management, systems engineering, hardware engineering, software engineering, and support) which are implemented in both development and maintenance projects.

As professionals, we need to use our own judgment and common sense to interpret the model for our organization. The process areas described in this model depict behaviors considered as best practices for most of the users.

Process areas and practices should be interpreted using an in-depth knowledge of CMMI-DEV, your organizational constraints, and your business environment.

1.1.2   Business Objectives in CMMI

Understanding the business objective is very important for every organization, and it plays a key role in enhancing an organization's continued existence. It can also improve its profitability and market share. Business objective can influence an organization's success; hence, organization objectives should be developed by senior management only. Some of the business objectives from CMMI-DEV include the following:

- Deliver products within budget and on time

- Improve productivity by a specified percent in a specified timeframe

- Maintain customer satisfaction ratings

- Improve time-to-market for new products or service releases by a specified percent in a specified timeframe

- Reduce the rate of product recalls by a specified percent in a specified timeframe

- Decrease the cost of maintaining legacy products by a specified percent in a specified timeframe

---

■ **Note**   To make the business objective more successful, pinpoint those areas that are most critical to the success of the organization.

CMMI talks about defining the organizational business objectives. There are several Specific Practices (SPs) where business objectives provide the principle context for interpreting and applying the practice. At all maturity levels, we have process areas that contain these practices. Business objective general practices (GPs) and SPs will be elaborated on at much greater length later in this book.

1.2   The Evolution of CMMI

Before you know when it was originated, shouldn't you know why it was originated? When the need for something becomes imperative, you are forced to find ways of getting or achieving it.

"Necessity is the mother of invention."

CMMI was originated by SEI (Software Engineering Institute) and sponsored by the US DOD (Department of Defense). The project consisted of members of industry, government, and Carnegie Mellon SEI. In the early 1980's, many US military projects involving software subcontractors were lagging behind the schedule.

Subcontractors were scattered both across the US and outside the US, and every organization had its own set of process guidelines to do the same work. Hence, it was difficult for DOD and NDIA (National Defense Industrial Association) to merge the output from multiple projects or from various vendors. A new working model was required which would enable every organization to follow the same path for building a new product or solution.

Capability Maturity Model (CMM) was developed based on the study and data collected from various organizations who had worked as a vendor with the U.S Department of Defense. In CMM, the term maturity refers to improving your processes on a continual basis.

At the request of the U.S. Air Force (USAF), Humphrey and SEI together created the process maturity framework to help the U.S. DOD to evaluate the software development process capability of their vendors, as part of the process of awarding them work contracts.

The full representation of Capability Maturity Model (CMM) was developed in 1991 and updated in 1993 as version 1.1.

In 2000, the CMMI team published the original CMMI Model for its training and appraisal method, which incorporated software and systems engineering. The design includes full support for the future integration of other disciplines.

The current version of the CMMI model at the time of writing is CMMI V1.3, which was released in 2010. Figure 1-1 visually represents the evolution of CMMI.

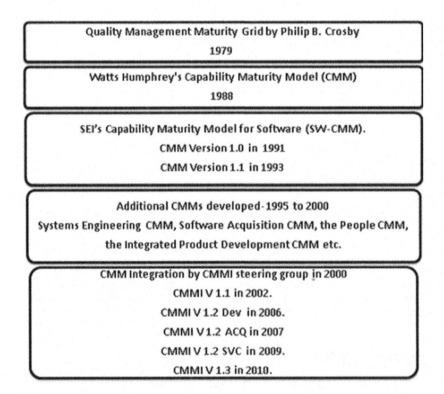

Figure 1-1. *The evolution of CMMI*

1.2.1   Why Use CMMI?

Here is an obvious question if you are new to CMMI: why should you use it? There are many reasons to choose CMMI, but and one of the most important is performance. The main purpose of CMMI is to improve the existing performance of organizational standards, processes, and procedures.

CMMI is also very helpful for the organizations that want to improve their capability to consistently and predictably deliver the products, services, and goods that its customers want. Hence, it also helps organizations to achieve its performance goals.

1.2.1.1   CMMI Is Used for Process Improvement

To cater to comprehensive business process improvements, CMMI features 25 different process areas. Each process area is composed of two kinds of goals (generic goal and specific goal) and two kinds of practices. There is also a lot of information for helping management to develop strategies.

In CMMI, there are three constellations to help improve a given business need, which are listed as follows:

- **Development:** For improving the development of solutions

- **Acquisition:** For improving the purchasing of products, services, and/or solutions

- **Services:** For improving the delivery of services and the creation of service systems to operate a solution

As mentioned previously, CMMI was written by a group of industry experts professionals. Consequently, the CMMI model comprises a set of industry best practices. IT organizations and industries use the CMMI model as a benchmark to improve their processes.

1.2.1.2   CMMI Is Used for Appraisals

Organizations also use CMMI to appraise the entire organization or just one business unit present at one or more locations. Appraisal is done using the best practices defined in the model.

This book covers both how to perform appraisal activities within your organization and how to determine who should be involved in the appraisal process.

1.3   Where CMMI Can Be Used?

CMMI can be used by any organization, small or large, that wants to improve its capabilities and performance. These days, CMMI is used across the organization and in fields as diverse as aviation and aerospace, computer networking, computer software, information technology, defense and space, hospital and healthcare, government administration, insurance, management consulting, outsourcing, and much more.

CMMI is also used by many commercial and government organizations to assist in defining the process improvements for system engineering, software engineering, and product and process development.

Many organizations use these processes to develop, acquire, and maintain products and services, as well as to benchmark themselves against other organizations. Better processes will lead to less rework, which reduces the overall cost and improves the quality of the product.

1.4   Who Can Use CMMI?

Many in the IT industry do not know whether they have a role to play in CMMI implementation. And if they do have a role to play, how do they initiate it?

Let's begin by looking at all the people who might be involved. This includes the CEO, the CTO, vice presidents, business unit heads, program managers, project managers, quality managers, team/tech leads, business analysts, system architects, designers, developers, testers, SQAs, configuration controllers, and training departments.

If you are connected to any of the aforementioned categories, then you are pretty much involved in the implementation of CMMI. In the future, there might be many more roles created with a connection to CMMI. But here's a more concise way to state who has a stake in CMMI: anybody who is involved in the planning and execution of an IT project—whether from engineering, project management, or support and process perspective—is involved in implementing CMMI practices.

1.4.1   CMMI Is Adopted Worldwide

Results published by CMMI Institute show that more than 1,900 appraisals in 61 countries were conducted in 2015, making it the fourth consecutive year for a record number of appraisals. The rate of growth has increased year over year, reaching 17% more appraisals in 2015 than in 2014 (see Figure 1-2).

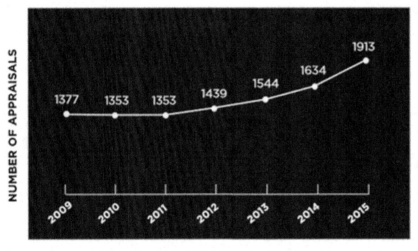

Figure 1-2. *The growth of CMMI appraisals*

CMMI is being adopted worldwide, including North America, Europe, India, Australia, Asia Pacific, and the Far East. CMMI is used by world's most admired organizations, including Samsung, Accenture, Proctor & Gamble, and Siemens.

This kind of response has substantiated the SEI's commitment to the CMMI models and SCAMPI. CMMI adoption has been a powerful differentiator for businesses and organizations, as well as a catalyst for economic growth for those who invest in its broad adoption.

> *"To compete in the global market, leaders must build organizations that can consistently deliver quality and value in products and services."*

—Kirk Botula, CEO of CMMI Institute.

1.5   About CMMI Institute

As part of its mission to transition mature technology to the software community, the SEI has transferred CMMI-related products and activities to the CMMI Institute, a 100%-controlled subsidiary of Carnegie Innovations, Carnegie Mellon University's technology-commercialization enterprise.

The CMMI Institute will conduct CMMI training and certification, sponsor conferences and classes, and provide information about CMMI process improvement models and appraisals.

CMMI Institute (`http://CMMIInstitute.com`) is the global leader in the advancement of best practices in people, process, and technology. The Institute provides tools and support for organizations that want to benchmark their capabilities, build maturity by comparing their operations to best practices, and identify performance gaps.

1.5.1   The CMMI Institute Partner Network

The CMMI Institute works with a network of CMMI Institute Partners, which are organizations and individuals trained and certified to provide official courses, appraisals, and consulting services.

The CMMI Institute Partner Network provides a vast, global reach to help us reach users, managers, and executives who can benefit from CMMI solutions. CMMI Institute Partners are the only source for authentic CMMI services outside the institute itself.

To find an authentic and licensed partner, you can search through the CMMI partner directory by browsing this link:

`http://partners.cmmiinstitute.com/find-partner-organization/`

You can also search the partners by geographic region and the product suite.

1.6   Summary

I hope that you now have an appreciation for the theoretical foundation for CMMI-DEV. In this chapter, we have discussed CMMI, both providing an overview and briefly reflecting on the business objective. We also covered the history of CMMI, why to use it, where it can be used, and who can use it.

In the next chapter, we will discuss about the design of CMMI, the levels within CMMI, and what they mean. We will also discuss process areas in CMMI, including they are mapped to each other.

CHAPTER 2

CMMI Design

In this chapter, we will focus on CMMI design, including how the CMMI Dev model is structured, how to interpret it, and why it is important to understand the design of CMMI.

The first question that comes to mind is, "Why it is important to understand CMMI design?"

To implement this model in your organization or projects, you need to follow a specific path which leads to the end goal. Once the path is understood, it becomes easy to interpret and execute.

Time is always an important factor and something we all want to save, so the next question that comes to mind is, "How easily can we understand and adapt this model?"

Let's start by breaking down the design of the CMMI DEV Model. What does CMMI stands for? And what is Development or DEV?

CMMI stands for Capability Maturity Model Integration:

- *Capability*: When we want to implement and achieve a process improvement in an individual process area.

- *Maturity*: When we want to implement and achieve process improvement in a set of process areas which are predefined.

- *Model*: Generated from the CMMI Framework.

- *Integration*: This approach uses a combination of selected models (e.g., CMMI for software, systems engineering, and integrated product development) that are integrated into the single framework, CMM-I. The "I" stands for integration. (The first model developed was CMMI for development).

2.1   CMMI Levels

In CMMI, each level describes the maturity of the process. Each maturity level consists of process areas (which are already defined), and these levels are achieved in a progressive manner.

Capability and maturity are associated with capability levels and maturity levels, respectively.

Both types of levels describe improvement paths to initiate CMMI implementation. So, how do we describe capability levels?

2.1.1   Capability Levels

A capability level is a path which ensures that an organization will improve an *individual* process area or a *group* of process areas incrementally. Focusing on the particulars of a given process will help an organization improve its capability level in that process area.

© Mukund Chaudhary 2017
M. Chaudhary and A. Chopra, *CMMI for Development*, DOI 10.1007/978-1-4842-2529-5_2

There are four capability levels:

- Level 0: Incomplete
- Level 1: Performed
- Level 2: Managed
- Level 3: Defined

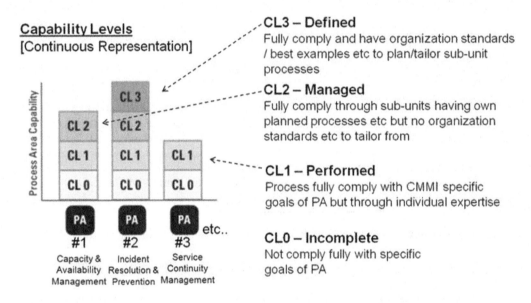

Figure 2-1. *Showing capability level continuous representation*

Let's interpret each capability level, one-by-one.

2.1.1.1 Capability Level 0: Incomplete

Incomplete means that specific goals are not satisfied for the process area. Also, generic goals do not exist for this level.

2.1.1.2 Capability Level 1: Performed

Performed means that needed work is accomplished and that specific goals of the process area are satisfied. At capability level 1, process improvements need to be institutionalized and maintained, or they may be lost completely over a period of time.

2.1.1.3   Capability Level 2: Managed

Managed means that your process has been planned and executed, as defined by your organization:

- Includes a team of skilled people

- Produces outputs in a controlled manner

- Involves the stakeholders

- Your process is monitored, controlled, and reviewed

- Includes an evaluation of your process description for process adherence

Process adherence at capability level 2 ensures that your organization retains existing practices during crucial times.

2.1.1.4   Capability Level 3: Defined

Defined means that tailoring of processes from your defined processes is done in the organization by adhering to its tailoring guidelines. (You will learn about *tailoring* later in the book.)

At capability level 3, organizations also contribute experiences to the organizational process assets that are gained during the implementation of processes.

You might wonder how you distinguish between capability levels 2 and 3. Let's look at the distinguishing factors:

> At capability level 2, either the complete process or some of its descriptions differ from one project to another. In other words, processes are not common throughout the organization.

> At capability level 3, standard processes are common throughout the organization. Processes are allowed to be tailored for a project or the organizational unit. Tailoring is done by following the defined tailoring guidelines for the organization.

At level 3, processes are written in a rigorous manner and are managed proactively. Processes are considered more consistent, and the only noticeable differences are allowed by the tailoring guidelines.

Once an organization achieves capability level 3 in the process areas that were considered for improvement, it can move ahead further on its process improvement path by focusing on implementing the high maturity process areas (i.e., Organizational Process Performance, Quantitative Project Management, Causal Analysis and Resolution, and Organizational Performance Management).

■ **Note**   Once an organization fulfills capability level 3 in process areas (i.e., OPP and QPM), then it should plan to move ahead and implement process areas CAR and OPM.

So far we have discussed the capability levels; now, let's look at the maturity levels.

2.1.2   Maturity Levels

A *maturity level* is a path that ensures organizations are able to improve their successive sets of process areas in an incremental manner. Each maturity level has a set of processes which, if implemented together, will help you to attain one full maturity level (e.g., to go from level 1 to level 2).

The five maturity levels progress from level 1 to level 5 in incremental stages (see Figure 2-2):

- Level 1: Initial
- Level 2: Managed
- Level 3: Defined
- Level 4: Quantitatively managed
- Level 5: Optimizing

CMMI Staged Represenation- Maturity Levels

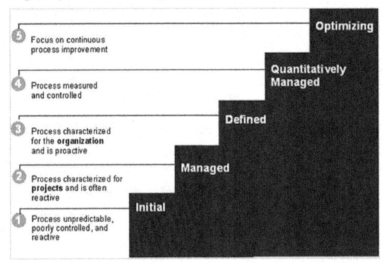

Figure 2-2. *Showing CMMI staged representations*

Let's interpret each maturity level.

2.1.2.1 Maturity Level 1: Initial

Initial means the processes are ad hoc. Success is dependent on the capability of a few people in the organization who are seen as heroes and not based on the available processes; in the future, when these few heroic people leave the organization, the team is unable to repeat the success.

In a maturity level 1 organization, the products built and services provided work well most of the time; however, the budget and schedule always get impacted and deviate from their documented plans.

Also, it has been observed that level 1 teams overcommit to their clients/customers. This is because, at times of crisis (e.g., an event that impacts the schedule), the whole team abandons the process in order to deliver faster. Due to this, they are unable to repeat the success.

2.1.2.2   Maturity Level 2: Managed

Managed means that projects are adhering to organization-defined processes. Team/resources working on the project possess the right skill levels to produce controlled outputs:

- Projects and their work products are monitored, controlled, and reviewed

- Projects and their work products are evaluated for adherence to their process descriptions

- Management is aware of the status of the work products at defined intervals (e.g., at major milestones and at the completion of major tasks)

- Commitments among relevant stakeholders are visible

■ **Note**   At maturity level 2, process discipline helps in ensuring the retention of existing practices during times of stress in the project. By following the process, projects are performed and managed as per the documented plans.

2.1.2.3   Maturity Level 3: Defined

Defined means that processes are well defined, documented, understood, and followed by various means (e.g., whether through procedures, methods or tools). Processes followed on a day-to-day basis are further improved over time at the organizational level:

- Processes at maturity level 3 help to establish a feeling among the team members that consistency is maintained in following the process across the organization or the business-unit level

- Projects perform tailoring on their defined processes as per the tailoring guidelines

Let's examine the distinguishing factors between maturity level 2 and 3.

At maturity level 2, the complete process or its descriptions can differ from one project to another. In other words, processes are not common throughout the organization.

At maturity level 3, standard processes are common across the organization. Processes can be tailored for one project or organizational unit by referring to the organization's defined tailoring guidelines.

Just as with capability level 3, the processes for maturity level 3 are written in a rigorous manner and managed proactively. Hence at level 3, processes are considered more consistent, and the only noticeable differences are allowed by the tailoring guidelines.

2.1.2.4   Maturity Level 4: Quantitatively Managed

Quantitatively managed means that an organization establishes objectives quantitatively for quality and process performance at both the organizational and project level. It then uses these quantitative objectives as criteria in managing projects:

- Quantitative objectives are defined by assessing the needs of the customer, end users, and organization and process implementers (Figure 2-3 shows an example of this where the measure schedule variance is -10% to 10%, and the measure effort variance is -15% to 15%)

- Quality and process performance objectives are viewed via statistical means and managed throughout the life of projects

- Process performance baselines and models are implemented that help to set the quality and process performance objectives; this will help an organization in achieving its business objectives

Business Objectives	Measure	Min Value	Max Value	Unit of Measure	Indicator Definition
To Deliver On Time	Schedule Variance	-10%	10%	Percentage	Extent to which number of days the delivery was varied from the planned delivery date (against planned and revised schedule)
To Deliver On Time	Effort Variance	-15%	15%	Percentage	Extent to which actual effort (measured in person hours) deviates from planned effort for a planned release/test cycle (against planned and revised effort)

Figure 2-3. *An example quantitative objective*

So, what is the critical distinguishing factor between maturity levels 3 and 4? At level 4, we can predict the process performance.

The project and selected subprocesses are controlled by using statistical and other quantitative techniques. Also, predictions are made by performing statistical analysis on the refined process data.

■ **Note** At maturity level 3, process performance cannot be predicted.

2.1.2.5   Maturity Level 5: Optimizing

Optimizing means that an organization focuses on improving its processes in a continuous manner by understanding its business objectives and performance needs (in quantitative terms).

Also, organizations use a quantitative approach to understand the variation inherent in the process and the causes of process outcomes:

- The goal is to improve the process performance by following an incremental and innovative approach

- Quality and process performance objectives are defined at the organizational level

- Defined processes and supporting technology combine to help organizations achieve the measurable improvements

Here are the critical distinguishing factors between maturity levels 4 and 5:

- At maturity level 4, the organizational and project teams understand and control performance at the subprocess level, and use these results to manage the projects

- At maturity level 5, the organization focuses on managing and improving organizational performance; this is ensured by collecting and analyzing the data from various projects

■ **Note** Be sure to collect data and perform analysis; this will help you to identify the gaps in process performance. Also, prepare a gap closure plan and take appropriate actions to ensure that organizational process improvement is measureable.

Let's summarize the comparison between Capability and Maturity Levels as depicted in the Table 2-1.

Table 2-1. *Comparing Capability and Maturity Levels*

Level	Continuous Representation Capability Levels	Staged Representation Maturity Levels
Level 0	Incomplete	
Level 1	Performed	Initial
Level 2	Managed	Managed
Level 3	Defined	Defined
Level 4		Quantitatively Managed
Level 5		Optimizing

■ **Note** The names used for the capability and maturity levels at levels 2 and 3 are similar in both representations (i.e., Managed and Defined).

2.1.3   An Approach for Process Improvement

Approaches for process improvement in CMMI are called *representations*; capability levels and maturity levels have their own respective representations:

- *Continuous*: a continuous representation approach leads us towards *capability levels*

- *Staged*: a staged representation approach leads us towards *maturity levels*

Now let's look at the structure of these representations (see Figures 2-4 and 2-5).

Continuous Representation

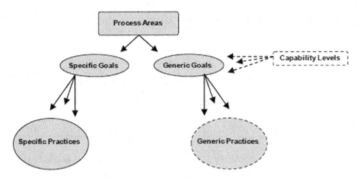

Figure 2-4. *Continuous representation*

Staged Representation

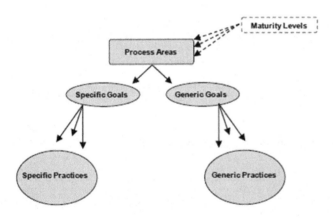

Figure 2-5. *Staged representation*

Looking at both representations reveals that the structure of continuous and staged representations is similar.

They contain similar components (e.g., process areas, specific goals, and specific practices) and have similar hierarchies.

In continuous representation, you can select a particular process area for improvement, along with the desired capability level for that process area.

In staged representation, you can select multiple process areas for improvement within a maturity level.

Based on our understanding of these levels, we can decide whether we want to proceed with a continuous (capability levels) or a staged (maturity levels) representation approach to implement CMMI DEV.

■ **Note** Both capability and maturity levels will lead to the same end result (i.e., process improvement).

To attain either a higher capability or maturity level, an organization needs to satisfy all the goals of a process area or a set of *process areas* from a given improvement perspective.

The Process Area boxes in the two figures lead us to an obvious question, "Is CMMI a process description?"

An important thing to bear in mind about CMMI as a model is that it is neither a process nor a description of the process.

For CMMI beginners, it has long been a misconception that CMMI is a process which we can follow and apply "AS IS" to the areas of an organization or its projects.

If CMMI is not a process, then what do we mean by Process Area?

In the CMMI model, a process area contains set of related *practices*. When these practices are implemented together, they satisfy the goals of the process area, which means that process improvement has been accomplished in that process area.

CMMI contains a set of different and unique process areas that are interconnected or have an inter-relationship with each other.

In the CMMI DEV Model, there are 22 process areas in total. (We will learn more about these process areas later in this and other chapters.)

You saw the terms *goals* and *practices* in both representations shown in Figures 2-4 and 2-5. Let's take a closer look at how they fit into CMMI.

As components (design) of CMMI, the terms goals and practices are present under each process area.

Let's visualize CMMI's structure first; we need to understand how process areas, goals, and practices are placed as components within CMMI.

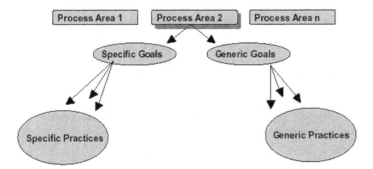

Figure 2-6. *How process areas, goals, and practices fit together*

And now let's look more specifically at goals and practices.

2.1.3.1   What Is a Specific Goal?

A *specific goal* (SG) is unique and present in each process area.

Under each specific goal, there are certain "specific practices" (SP). When we implement the specific practices successfully, then we satisfy the specific goal. Once all the specific goals are satisfied, it means the process area is satisfied.

During CMMI appraisals, specific goals are evaluated to check whether the process area is satisfied.

2.1.3.2   What Is a Specific Practice?

A *specific practice* is the activity description; when a specific practice is implemented, it helps to achieve the associated specific goal (see Figure 2-7).

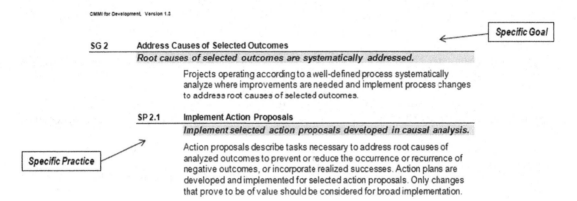

Figure 2-7.   *A specific goal and practice*

2.1.3.3   What Is a Generic Goal?

Generic goals are called "generic" because they have the same goal statement, which is common across all 22 process areas.

Generic goals are used during the CMMI appraisals to evaluate whether a process area is satisfied or not satisfied.

2.1.3.4   What Is a Generic Practice?

A *generic practice* is called such because it is the same practice that is used across all 22 process areas.

A generic practice is present under generic goals. A generic practice contains an activity description that, once implemented, helps in achieving the generic goal of a process area (see Figure 2-8).

CMMI for Development, Version 1.3

GG 2   Institutionalize a Managed Process

The process is institutionalized as a managed process.   Generic Goal

GP 2.1   Establish an Organizational Policy

Generic Practice   Establish and maintain an organizational policy for planning and
performing the process.

The purpose of this generic practice is to define the organizational
expectations for the process and make these expectations visible to those
members of the organization who are affected. In general, senior
management is responsible for establishing and communicating guiding
principles, direction, and expectations for the organization.

Not all direction from senior management will bear the label "policy." The
existence of appropriate organizational direction is the expectation of this
generic practice, regardless of what it is called or how it is imparted.

CAR Elaboration

This policy establishes organizational expectations for identifying and
systematically addressing causal analysis of selected outcomes.

CM Elaboration

Generic Practice   This policy establishes organizational expectations for establishing and
Elaboration   maintaining baselines, tracking and controlling changes to work products
(under configuration management), and establishing and maintaining
integrity of the baselines.

Figure 2-8. *A generic goal and practice*

Visually, the structure of generic goals and generic practices looks like a grid, where the different levels
are shown horizontally and the specific goals within that level are shown as a vertical list of boxes with
incremented numbers (see Figure 2-9).

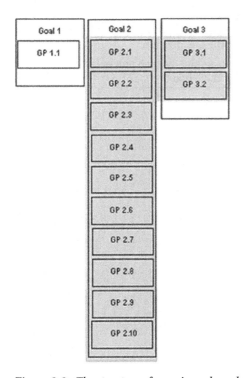

Figure 2-9. *The structure of generic goals and generic practices*

Table 2-2 describes the specific goals and practices for each level, interpreting what each means.

Table 2-2. *A Description and Interpretation of Each Generic Goal and Generic Practice Under It*

Generic Goal	Description	Generic Practice	Description	Interpretation
GG1	Achieve Specific Goals	GP 1.1	Perform Specific Practices	To fulfill or satisfy this generic practices build and to deliver the expected work output by following the processes.
				What this means:
				In this practice, it is not "mandatory" to follow a documented process or plan.
				Hence, it also can be done "Informally."
GG2	Institutionalize a Managed Process	GP 2.1	Establish an Organizational Policy	To fulfill or satisfy this generic practice, we have to define or set the expectations of the process at the organizational level.
				What this means:
				We have to define the policy for all process areas (e.g., Project Planning and Requirements Management) which we are implementing in our organization.
				Doing this ensures that the policy is visible to all those who could be affected (e.g., Senior Management and Project delivery teams).
				In other words, everyone involved in the organization commits to following and executing their processes as defined in the organization.
				Note: Policy examples for each process area are covered later in the book.

(*continued*)

Table 2-2. (*continued*)

Generic Goal	Description	Generic Practice	Description	Interpretation
		GP 2.2	Plan the Process	To fulfill or satisfy this generic practice, we have to identify all parameters that would be required to perform the process.
				What this means:
				In simple terms, we must have a plan to execute the process.
				What should the plan include? Here are some examples:
				• A written process to guide how the process needs to be executed
				• Requirements for developing the work products
				• A plan for managing dependencies (i.e., tasks, resources, etc.)
				• A plan for managing resources (i.e., SW, HW, people, etc.)
				• A plan for managing relevant stakeholders
				• A plan for risk management
				• A plan for training
				• A plan for project monitoring and control
				• A plan for management reviews
				Once the plan is prepared, we need to ensure that the plan is reviewed and agreed to by all the stakeholders. It is an important activity because, when we perform the process, we do not perform it alone. It is performed by multiple people.
				Hence, all stakeholders must be committed to the plan.

(*continued*)

Table 2-2. (*continued*)

Generic Goal	Description	Generic Practice	Description	Interpretation
		GP 2.3	Provide Resources	To fulfill or satisfy this generic practice, we have to ensure that all the required resources are made available to perform the process. *What this means*:
				We have to plan, monitor and arrange the required resources whenever their use is planned. Resource types could be infrastructure (i.e., a facility, software, hardware, etc.), people, tools, and so on. To execute and satisfy all the process areas, resources are necessary.
		GP 2.4	Assign Responsibility	To fulfill or satisfy this generic practice, we must ensure that people are accountable for the processes they perform. This includes achieving the desired results of that process.
				What this means:
				We have to clearly define and assign the responsibility to people to perform specific process and tasks.
				We have to ensure that people understand and also accept their responsibilities.
				One approach for assigning a responsibility is to assign it through job descriptions or documented plans.
		GP 2.5	Train People	To fulfill or satisfy this generic practice, we have to ensure people possess right skills and expertise in performing or supporting the process.
				What this means:
				We need to analyze the skills and expertise of our team members. And upon analysis, if we find a gap in the required skill level, we need to plan and deliver the necessary training to our team members to bridge the gap.
				Hence, training people is important. People must have the requisite skills for performing a process in order to achieve the desired results.
				For every process area in the CMMI model, people should be trained to perform it.
				In organizations, training delivery is managed by the separate training team/department.
				Provided training might include on-the-job training, mentoring, classroom training, and so on.

(*continued*)

Table 2-2. (*continued*)

Generic Goal	Description	Generic Practice	Description	Interpretation
		GP 2.6	Control Work Products	To fulfill or satisfy this generic practice, we must manage and control the integrity of certain work products. These are identified in the project plan for executing the process.
				What this means:
				When we prepare the plan to perform the process, at that time we also have to identify all the work products which would be produced and are required to be put under configuration management.
				Controlling the work product here means work products are version controlled with proper naming conventions, they have a baseline, they are access controlled, and so on.
		GP 2.7	Identify and Involve Relevant Stakeholders	To fulfill or satisfy this generic practice, we have to ensure that relevant stakeholders are available and participating during the execution of the process.
				What this means:
				We have to identify all the relevant stakeholders during the planning of the process, and then monitor their participation at regular intervals.
				Phases where stakeholders could be involved include the following:
				• Planning
				• Decision making
				• Commitments
				• Reviews
				• Defining requirements
				• Problem resolutions

(*continued*)

Table 2-2. (*continued*)

Generic Goal	Description	Generic Practice	Description	Interpretation
		GP 2.8	Monitor and Control the Process	To fulfill or satisfy this generic practice, we have to ensure that the process is monitored and controlled on a daily basis.
				Doing this gives us visibility into the execution of the process; whenever required, corrective actions can be taken.
				What this means:
				After performing the process, we have to do the following tasks:
				• Assess the actual progress against the plan
				• Evaluate accomplishments and the results achieved
				• Evaluate deviations against the plan
				• Identify issues in executing the process
				• Discuss the results and status with management
		GP 2.9	Objectively Evaluate Adherence	To fulfill or satisfy the generic practice, we need to ensure that the process is implemented as planned.
				What this means:
				Identify people who are *not* responsible for performing the process activities which need to be evaluated.
				This is necessary for an unbiased evaluation.
				The people identified will evaluate the process performance at regular intervals and will confirm adherence by publishing the results.
				Corrective actions will be required when there is any issue observed in process adherence.
		GP 2.10	Review Status with Higher Level Management	To fulfill or satisfy this generic practice, we have to ensure that the management team has sufficient visibility into the process performance.
				What this means:
				We have to report the progress of the process execution, including its results (i.e., actual vs. planned). Management must also be informed of any risks or issues.
				Doing this ensures that any support or action needed from management can be executed in a timely manner, without any last-minute surprises.
				The management team could include program managers, delivery heads, or VPs.

(*continued*)

Table 2-2. (*continued*)

Generic Goal	Description	Generic Practice	Description	Interpretation
GG3	Institutionalize a Defined Process	GP 3.1	Establish a Defined Process	To fulfill or satisfy this generic practice, we have to ensure that the organization has defined processes which could also be tailored according to the needs of the specific project instance.
				What this means:
				We have defined the processes covering all the process areas of the CMMI Dev model which an organization wants to implement.
				We have defined the tailoring guidelines, which can be used to tailor any process whenever the need arises.
				We must maintain the tailoring records, and we must update the processes whenever necessary.
		GP 3.2	Collect Process Related Experiences	To fulfill or satisfy this generic practice, we have to ensure that process-related experiences are collected.
				What this means:
				During the process planning and process execution phases, we must observe new experiences.
				Those experiences that we collect will help us to analyze the process activities, and then categorize them as mistakes or best practices. We can also call them lessons learned and process improvement suggestions.
				Publishing such experiences might help other organization members who will work on a similar process in the future. These future workers can benefit from the lessons learned.

2.2   Process Areas

Process areas are viewed differently in the two representations. Figures 2-10 and 2-11 show the use of process areas in continuous and staged representations, respectively.

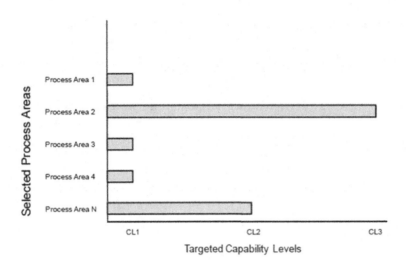

Figure 2-10. *Process areas in continuous representation*

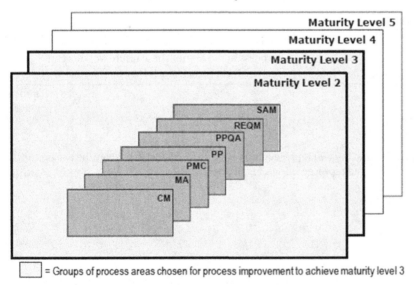

Figure 2-11. *Visualizing process areas in staged representation*

In continuous representation, process areas are divided into four categories:

- Process management

- Project management

- Engineering

- Support

When process areas are selected for implementation, check and analyze the maturity level to be attained for the process area (i.e., select the appropriate capability level).

For example, assume an organization decides to achieve capability level 2 for one process area and capability level 3 for another process area.

Once an organization achieves a capability level, it should always target achieving the next capability level in the same process areas or target a larger number of process areas.

For example, once an organization attains capability level 3 in almost all of the process areas, then the next step for that organization should be to plan and attain high maturity process areas and track the capability of each through capability level 3.

So, how should an organization select process areas combined with their required capability levels?

This is described in a *target profile*, which defines the process areas that need to be addressed and the capability levels targeted for each. It also describes the goals and practices the organization will have to address in its process-improvement efforts.

In staged representation, process areas are grouped into maturity levels that indicate which process areas will be implemented to achieve each maturity level.

For example, at maturity level 2, a predefined set of process areas might require an organization to achieve all the goals of all the process areas.

Once maturity level 2 is achieved, the organization's focus should be on achieving maturity level 3 process areas, and so on.

Generic goals present in each process area are predefined. Generic goal 2 is applicable to maturity level 2, and generic goal 3 is applicable to maturity levels 3 through 5.

2.3 Mapping Process Areas

In CMMI, process areas are mapped into four categories, along with their defined maturity levels.

These four categories include the following:

- Project management

- Engineering

- Support

- Process Management

You might wonder why there are only four categories. Why not five, or perhaps six? What you need to keep in mind is that the CMMI model was designed by a team of industry experts who have considered these issues from all possible scenarios and perspectives.

We will cover these process areas later in the book, at which time it will be easier to see how these process areas relate to the aforementioned four categories.

Figure 2-12 shows a lot of useful information, including process areas and their abbreviations. It also includes a category column that explains which category a given process area belongs to, and a maturity column that tells us roughly which maturity level a given process area is placed in according to the CMMI Dev Model.

Process Area	Abbreviation	Category	Maturity Level
Causal Analysis and Resolution	CAR	Support	5
Configuration Management	CM	Support	2
Decision Analysis and Resolution	DAR	Support	3
Integrated Project Management	IPM	Project Management	3
Measurement and Analysis	MA	Support	2
Organizational Process Definition	OPD	Process Management	3
Organizational Process Focus	OPF	Process Management	3
Organizational Performance Management	OPM	Process Management	5
Organizational Process Performance	OPP	Process Management	4
Organizational Training	OT	Process Management	3
Product Integration	PI	Engineering	3
Project Monitoring and Control	PMC	Project Management	2
Project Planning	PP	Project Management	2
Process and Product Quality Assurance	PPQA	Support	2
Quantitative Project Management	QPM	Project Management	4
Requirements Development	RD	Engineering	3
Requirements Management	REQM	Project Management	2
Risk Management	RSKM	Project Management	3
Supplier Agreement Management	SAM	Project Management	2
Technical Solution	TS	Engineering	3
Validation	VAL	Engineering	3
Verification	VER	Engineering	3

Figure 2-12. *Process areas and their maturity level*

Process areas are assigned into the following categories:

1. Project Management (seven total process areas)

   - Project planning (PP)

   - Integrated project management (IPM)

   - Project monitoring and control (PMC)

   - Requirements management (REQM)

   - Risk management (RSKM)

- Supplier agreement management (SAM)
- Quantitative project management (QPM)

2. Engineering (Five Total Process Areas)
    - Requirements development (RD)
    - Technical solution (TS)
    - Product integration (PI)
    - Validation (VAL)
    - Verification (VER)

3. Process management (five total process areas)
    - Organizational performance management (OPM)
    - Organizational process definition (OPD)
    - Organizational process focus (OPF)
    - Organizational process performance (OPP)
    - Organizational training (OT)

■ **Note**   All of the process management process areas start with *Organizational*.

---

4. Support (five total process areas)

    - Causal analysis and resolution (CAR)
    - Configuration management (CM)
    - Decision analysis and resolution (DAR)
    - Measurement and analysis (MA)
    - Process and product quality assurance (PPQA)

The next step is to walk through each process area under each category.

The first category is Project Management. These process areas contain best practices for the roles to be played by the project manager or program manager in an organization.

2.3.1   Project Planning

The Project Planning (PP) process area covers the best practices related to the following:

- Estimates
    - Project scope (through WBS or a tasks list)
    - Effort and cost (based on size)
- Project life cycle phases
    - Based on the requirements scope, these define life cycle phases

- Preparation of the project plan

  - Prepare a schedule

  - Identify risks

  - Manage data

  - Plan your resources (staff, equipment, infrastructure facility, process/SOPs, etc.)

  - Plan for training (based on the requirements/Technology gaps)

  - Plan for stakeholder involvement

- Obtain commitment on the project plan

  - Here, we need commitment from everyone on the plan who is responsible for executing the plan; this includes project team members, management, and various other internal departments (e.g., IT infrastructure, HR and training, and network)

  - We need to identify those plans that can affect the project, as well as to ensure that these plans are reviewed with the relevant stakeholders

  - Based on the reviews, we need to revisit the plan and fix the gaps if there are any differences between estimates and resources

2.3.2   Integrated Project Management

The Integrated Project Management (IPM) process area covers the best practices related to focusing on project-defined process:

- Create the project-defined process by referring to all QMS processes

- The project-defined process should be able to meet and deliver the project requirements (e.g., product-life processes such as engineering and support)

- There could be a need to tailor the processes from the organization's standard processes

- While forming the defined process, ensure that various factors are considered

  - Stakeholder requirements and commitment

  - Operational and business environment

  - Organization processes and tailoring guidelines

2.3.3   Project Monitoring and Control

The Project Monitoring and Control (PMC) process area covers the best practices related to the following:

- Monitor the project against the plan

  - Track the schedule (planned vs. actual completion of activities and milestones)

  - Track the effort, cost, and size (planned vs. actual)

  - Identify and analyze deviations from the plan (schedule, effort, and cost)

- Track resources (e.g., staff, processes, computers, software, infrastructure, and facilities)

- Track the current skills of team members vs. the required skills set (i.e., plan and track the training conducted)

- Monitor commitments

  - Track internal and external people commitments (i.e., planned vs. actual completion of commitments) and focus on commitments which are about to be missed or not fulfilled

  - Maintain records of commitment reviews (e.g., meeting minutes and status reports)

- Monitor project risks

  - Track risks on a regular basis (for risks documented in the risk register)

  - Update risk status in the risk register (e.g., some risks may no longer be a risk, or a given risk's severity might increase from medium to high)

  - Report risk status in a timely manner to relevant stakeholders (i.e., in status meetings, status reports, etc.)

- Monitor data management (e.g., employ data management activities tracking, as planned in the project plan)

- Monitor stakeholder involvement

  - Track stakeholder involvement (i.e., managers, staff, customers, end users, suppliers, etc., as planned in the project plan)

  - Re-plan stakeholder involvement (based on any changes or updates in the status of the requirements)

- Conduct progress reviews

  - Conduct project reviews and communicate progress updates to relevant stakeholders on a regular basis (as planned in the project plan)

  - Document change requests and track them to closure

  - Perform milestone reviews

  - Conduct milestone reviews with relevant stakeholders at planned intervals or phases (i.e., to ensure progress is made as per the plan)

  - Review the schedule, effort, milestone deliverables, planned commitments, and any risks

  - Manage corrective action to closure

  - Identify and collect issues for which action is required (these can be taken from the various project reviews performed)

  - Analyze and plan corrective action

  - Take corrective action (review the action to be taken with the stakeholders)

  - Analyze the results of a given corrective action (for effective implementation)

  - Document any identified deviation from the planned results and plan for closure

2.3.4   Requirements Management

The Requirements Management (REQM) process area covers the best practices related to the following:

- Understand the requirements

  - To evaluate and accept requirements, establish clear criteria (to avoid rework and customer rejections)

  - Perform requirements analysis and evaluate requirements against the set criteria

  - Ensure that the requirements set is approved

- Obtain commitment to the requirements

  - Perform impact assessment on requirement changes (to assess the impact on commitments to existing requirements)

  - Ensure that requirement commitments are available whenever any change in a requirement comes or when a new requirement is added

- Manage requirement changes

  - Ensure that requirement changes are documented (maintain a change history)

  - Maintain requirement change impact reports

  - Ensure that the requirements database is accessible to all relevant stakeholders

- Maintain bidirectional traceability of requirements (e.g., a traceability matrix to ensure that a requirement is tracked from its source to its lower level requirements—and back again from the lower level to the source requirement)

- Ensure there is alignment between project work and the requirements

  - Identify and document any inconsistencies found between project plans and the requirements

  - Update plans (if required due to changes in the requirements baseline)

2.3.5   Risk Management

The Risk Management (RSKM) process area covers the best practices related to the following:

- Prepare for risk management (i.e., document the risk management strategy, categorizing risks and defining parameters to evaluate and control risks)

- Determine risk sources and categories

  - Identify and prepare a source list of risks (i.e., a list of internal and external sources)

    - Uncertain requirements

    - Unavailable technology

    - Cost or funding issues

- Identify and prepare risk categories (for organizing risks)
  - Project phases (e.g., requirements, design, coding, and testing)
  - Project management risks (e.g., budget risks, schedule risks, and resource risks)
- Determine risk parameters (e.g., risk likelihood, risk consequences, and defining threshold values for risk categories)
  - Risk likelihood indicates the probability of a risk occurring
  - Risk consequence describes the impact and severity of a risk occurring
  - Defining threshold values for each risk category identifies when to trigger mitigation or a contingency plan
- Identify and analyze risks
  - Identify and document risks (e.g., risks related to cost, schedule, and performance)
  - Review WBS and the project plan when identifying risks
    - Reviewing WBS ensures that work effort related risks are identified
    - Reviewing the project plan ensures that all project related risks are identified
- Evaluate, categorize, and prioritize risks
  - Once the risk list is ready, evaluate each risk using defined parameters
    - Likelihood of the risk occurring (unlikely, likely, almost certain, etc.)
    - Impact if the risk occurs (high, medium, or low)
    - Severity if the risk occurs (high, medium or low)
    - Threshold
  - Categorize and prioritize each risk for mitigation
- Mitigate risks
  - Develop mitigation plans for risks (select risks to proactively reduce their potential impact)
  - Develop risk contingency plans
  - Assign responsibility to track and address each identified risk
- Implement risk mitigation plans (and then monitor the status of the risk once the mitigation plan is initiated)

2.3.6   Supplier Agreement Management

Use supplier agreement management (SAM) when the development of the product or one component of the product is not done by the project team, yet the team is responsible for delivering that product or component to the client.

The Supplier Agreement Management process area covers the best practices related to establishing supplier agreements:

- Determine the acquisition type for a product or a component of the product
    - Purchase modified COTS products
    - Obtain the product (or component) through supplier agreement
    - Obtain the product (or component) from an in-house supplier
    - Obtain the product (or component) from the customer
    - Obtain the product (or component) from a preferred supplier
- Select suppliers
    - Before selecting any supplier, it is important to evaluate suppliers based on their ability or past experience in delivering the required product or product component
    - Maintain a list of candidate suppliers
    - Maintain a list of preferred suppliers
    - Maintain records that evaluate the suppliers (i.e., the proposals evaluated, the basis of selecting a candidate supplier, and the advantages and disadvantages of each)
- Establish and maintain supplier agreements
    - Create a written agreement between the organization and the supplier (i.e., a statement of work, a contract, etc.)
    - Provide an overview of the work to be done in the written agreement
    - Draft the agreement based on the type of work (and insert language based on what you feel is right)
    - Agreements are usually reviewed by the legal/advisory team
- Include things in your agreement that fit your organization's needs; typical things to include might be the following:
    - Establish a statement of work, including terms and conditions, deliverables, schedule, and product acceptance procedures
    - Document who is responsible and authorized to make changes to the supplier agreement
    - Document a requirements change management procedure
    - Document procedures to be followed by the supplier
    - Document when reviews will be done with the supplier
    - Document responsibilities of the supplier during the maintenance period

2.3.7   Satisfy Supplier Agreements

An organization should perform activities with the supplier as documented in the written agreement. On a regular basis, it should track the supplier work status and performance (i.e., track the schedule, effort, and cost). It should also maintain progress reports and review the processes being used by the supplier in delivering the product.

Before accepting the acquired product, an organization should evaluate and accept the deliverables shared by the supplier, as per the set acceptance criteria in the agreement. An organization should also share the feedback/bugs/action points with the supplier if deliverables shared are unacceptable or need corrections.

2.3.8   Ensure a Transition of Products

There should be a smooth transition when the final deliverable/product is transferred to the organization by the supplier. Hence, the transition plan should be prepared and agreed upon by the organization and the supplier. What follows are the points to be ensured during the product transition:

- Ensure that the required facility is available to receive and store the product

- Ensure that training is planned and conducted for the people responsible for receiving, storing, and maintaining the product (i.e., the product should be maintained as per the supplier agreement and license terms)

- Ensure that the transition plan is monitored and transition report is shared with the relevant stakeholders for the status update

2.3.9   Quantitative Project Management (QPM)

The purpose of the Quantitative Project Management (QPM) process area is to manage the project in quantitative terms (see Figure 2-13); doing so will help the organization to achieve the project's established quality and process performance objectives:

- Prepare for quantitative management

- Define a project's objectives

- Define measurable quality and process performance objectives for the project

- Document the project's objectives

  - Objectives should detail the needs and priorities of the customer, end users, and other relevant stakeholders

  - Objectives should be specific, measurable, attainable, relevant, and time-bound

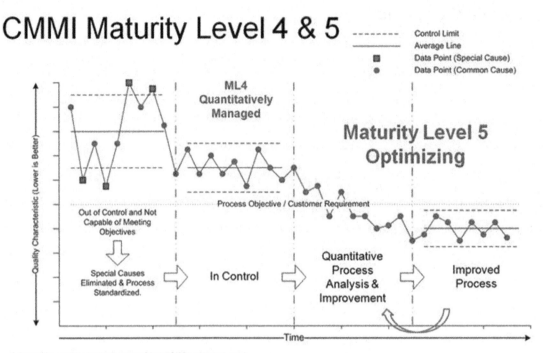

Figure 2-13. *Documenting the process objectives*

- Measure the quality of the project's attributes

    - The mean time between failures

    - The cycle time

    - The defect escape rates

- Proactively identify risks, such as the chance that the project's quality and process performance objectives will not be met

- If there are conflicts among the project's quality and process performance objectives, ensure that they have been resolved (e.g., if one objective cannot be achieved without compromising another)

- Maintain traceability from the source to the project's quality and process performance objectives

- The sources subject to tracing can be highly varied

    - The organization's quality and process performance objectives

    - The customer's quality objectives

    - The business objectives

- Maintain the following documents

  - The quality and process performance objective sheet

  - The project defined process (defines how the project will be able to achieve its quality and process performance objectives)

  - Defined criteria for evaluating process alternatives for the project

- Defined criteria can include the following:

  - Quality and process performance objectives

  - Project lifecycle models

  - Stakeholder requirements

- Identify alternative processes and subprocesses for the project

  - Analysis of process performance baselines (created at the organization level) can help in identifying subprocesses that will facilitate achieving the project's quality and process performance objectives

  - Subprocesses could also be identified from the organization's set of standard processes

  - Alternative subprocesses that best meet the criteria should be selected

- Select measures and analytic techniques

  - Common measures that support the quantitative management should be identified from the organizational process assets

  - Measures which could be used to manage the subprocesses should be identified

  - Specify the operational definitions of measures, their collection points in subprocesses, and how the integrity of measures will be determined

  - Identify the statistical and other quantitative techniques to be used in quantitative management

  - Determine what process performance baselines and models may be needed to support identified analyses

- Maintain the following documents

  - Definitions of measures and analytic techniques to be used in quantitative management

  - Traceability of measures back to the project's quality and process performance objectives

  - Quality and process performance objectives for selected subprocesses and their attributes

  - Process performance baselines and models for use by the project

- Quantitatively manage the project
    - Monitor the performance of selected subprocesses using statistical and other quantitative techniques
    - Collect data, as defined by the selected measures, on the subprocesses as they execute
    - Monitor the variation and stability of the selected subprocesses and address deficiencies
    - Monitor the capability and performance of the selected subprocesses, and then address deficiencies

2.3.10   Engineering Process Areas

So far we have covered Project Management process areas. Next, we'll look at the second category of process areas, Engineering. These process areas contain best practices for the roles to be played by the business/ requirements analyst, the architect, GUI designers, technical/functional leads, and developers and testers in an organization.

2.3.10.1   Requirements Development

The focus of the Requirements Development (RD) process area is to collect and analyze requirements. We can segregate requirements into three different types:

- Customer Requirements
- Product Requirements
- Product Component Requirements

RD covers the best practices related to developing customer requirements.

2.3.10.2   Developing the Customer Requirements

Here we need to elicit requirements from all the stakeholders' points of view. It's important to understand their needs and expectations. Also, we need to proactively identify those requirements which are not communicated or provided by the client/stakeholder, but are essential for the product or product component delivery.

We can use the following techniques to elicit the requirements:

- Interview sessions
- Prototypes
- Brainstorming
- Market surveys
- Use cases

Documents to be maintained include the following:

- Requirement Q&As
- Prototypes
- Survey results
- Meeting minutes

2.3.10.3   Transform the Stakeholder Needs into Customer Requirements

For building customer requirements, you need to consolidate all the inputs/information received from all stakeholders, but also do the following:

- Check whether any information is missing, and update the missing part
- Determine whether any conflicts exist in the requirements

In scenarios where the customer provides only the set of requirements, the customer requirements could conflict with the needs and expectations of the relevant stakeholders. Hence, it is important to resolve the conflict before treating customer requirements as a recognized set of requirements.

Documents to be maintained include documented customer requirements (i.e., a business requirements specification).

2.3.10.4   Develop the Product Requirements

You'll need to analyze the customer requirements to arrive at detailed product requirements:

- Establish product and product component requirements
- Associate the requirements with product life cycle phases

In scenarios where we chose to follow an iterative or incremental development model, the requirements must be allocated to iterations or increments based on the following criteria:

- Customer priorities
- Technology related issues
- Project objectives

You will also need to document customer functional and quality attributes requirements. This will help when describing what the product will do. Functional requirements have to be described in technical terms, to create the product design.

Examples of quality attribute measures include the following:

- Production of a simple report shall take less than 20 seconds for 95% of the cases
- The system shall be able to process 100 payment transactions per second in peak load

Documents to be maintained include documented technical requirements (i.e., a software requirements specification)

2.3.10.5   Allocate the Product Component Requirements

Next, we will need to allocate the product component requirements; these include the following tasks:

- Allocate requirements to functions

- Allocate requirements to each product components

- Capture design constraints for the product and product components

- Allocate requirements to the delivery increments

2.3.10.6   Identify the Interface Requirements

We will also need to identify interfaces between the functions, as well as ensure that interfaces identified are both external and internal to the product. Also, we need to ensure that requirements are developed for the identified interfaces (e.g., the data characteristics of the software).

2.3.10.7   Analyze and Validate Requirements

We must also validate requirements to ensure that the product being produced will perform as intended in the environment it is supposed to perform in. As the name suggests, this is simply a matter of validating our requirements and helping us prevent the cost of failure.

2.3.10.8   Establish Operational Concepts and Scenarios

We need to document operational concepts and scenarios (i.e., the sequence of events that might occur during product development, deployment, delivery, support (including maintenance and sustainment), training, and disposal.

This means we need to define the environment in which the product or product component will operate, including its boundaries and constraints. One aspect of this is creating use cases.

We also need to establish a definition of required functionality and quality attributes. A functional definition can include actions, sequence, inputs, outputs, or other information that communicates the manner in which the product will be used. Quality attributes can also be important from business needs perspective, and they serve as an input to the design process.

Documents to be maintained include the following:

- Definitions of the required functionality and quality attributes (document these in the SRS)

- Activity diagrams and use cases (document these in the SRS)

2.3.10.9   Analyze the Requirements

Review that the requirements are complete, feasible, realizable, and verifiable. Ensure that any risk assessment conducted with respect to the requirements is documented.

Documents to be maintained include the following:

- A requirements review defects report

- A requirements clarification report

- A risk register

- A risk section could also be added in the SRS

2.3.10.10   Validate the Requirements

You also need to ensure that the requirements are validated by the client/end user before initiating the design/development work. It is important to instill confidence in the client that the requirements collected/defined will be delivered as required in the product.

Examples of validation techniques include prototypes, demonstration/product presentation, simulations, and so on.

The documents to be maintained include the following:

- Documented prototypes

- Presentations

- Meeting minutes

2.3.10.11   Technical Solution

The focus of the technical solution is to design and implement solutions according to the requirements. The Technical Solution (TS) process area covers the best practices related to selecting component solutions, which includes the following tasks:

- Develop solutions for design alternatives that feature current vs. new technologies, COTS products, tools and so on, as required to implement the requirements (there will always be more than one possible solution to implement a requirement)

- Develop the criteria to select the best solution from the multiple alternatives available (i.e., criteria examples are cost, time, product performance, etc.)

- Document the selection criteria for selecting the best/final option among the available alternatives list (i.e., the reasons for selecting a particular option/solution)

Documents to be maintained include reports that evaluate the design, new technology, COTS products, tools, and so on.

Here are a couple things to keep in mind when developing the design:

- Employ techniques and methods known for producing effective design (e.g., prototypes, structural models, object oriented design, and entity relationship models)

- Ensure that design standards are adhered to while preparing the design

Documents to be maintained include the following:

- Product architecture

- Design standards

To establish a technical data package, you need to document the required product components levels:

- The subsystem

- Hardware configuration items

- Computer software configuration items

- Computer software product components

Documents to be maintained include those related to developing high- and low-level design.

Follow these criteria when designing interfaces:

- Define the interface criteria
- Identify the interfaces associated with other product components and external items
- Apply the interface criteria to the design alternatives
- Document the selected interface designs and the rationale for the selection

Documents to be maintained include the following:

- The interfaces in high- and low-level design
- The interfaces evaluation report (i.e., the DAR record)

2.3.10.12 Perform Make, Buy, or Reuse Analyses

Make, buy or reuse analysis is done to determine which product or product component needs to be acquired as part of the project/product delivery. The purpose of this analysis is to understand which product or product component cannot or should not be developed in-house, whether due to its high complexity, the lack of skills of your team members, or any other reasons.

It is also possible that some product or product component is already available as part of the delivery of past projects, and that it could be reused in the current product development.

Hence, by acquiring or reusing product components, you can save time and effort developing the current product or component.

In that vein, we need to do the following:

- Define criteria for when to reuse a product component
- Analyze designs to determine if a product or component should be developed, reused, or purchased

Documents to be maintained include a make, buy, or reuse analysis report. This document should describe how to implement a product design to develop software code. Examples of software coding methods include the following:

- Structured programming
- Object oriented programming
- Automatic code generation
- Software code reuse

During the software code development, the organization needs to adhere to the appropriate coding standards (e.g., language standards like .net and Java) and take these steps to ensure quality control:

- Plan and perform software code peer reviews
- Perform unit testing

Documents to be maintained include the following:

- Source code
- Coding methods
- Coding standards

- Peer review reports

- Unit test cases

- Results

2.3.10.13 Develop Product Support Documentation

To install, operate, and maintain the product, you'll also need to provide support documentation to the client. Documents to be maintained include the following:

- User manual

- Maintenance manual

- End user training material

- Online help

2.3.10.14 Product Integration

The purpose of product integration (PI) is to assemble and integrate the product from the product components. We need to ensure that the integrated product behaves properly before we deliver it to the client. Product integration can be done in two ways:

- All the product components can be integrated, tested, and delivered to the client

- The components can be integrated in incremental stages (e.g., if an iterative model is used for product development, then the continuous integration path could be followed to assemble the product components)

The Product Integration process area covers the best practices related to preparing for PI:

- Prepare and maintain an integration strategy

- Product components are available to facilitate product integration

  - Integration has to be conducted in a single build or in incremental builds

  - An integration procedure is defined

  - Features need to be tested in each iteration/build when using iterative development

  - Interfaces need to be managed

  - An integration environment needs to be created

  - Testing tools/equipment need to be created

  - Test results/reports need to be created and evaluated

- Evaluate and select the best integration strategy to be adopted

  - Evaluate and choose the best integration strategy method from the options available (use the DAR method for evaluation)

  - Upon selection of the best option according to you, document the reasons for selecting the option

Documents to be maintained include the following:

- The product integration strategy
- The DAR record (for evaluating the options for the integration method)

Follow these steps to create the product integration environment:

- Assess the requirements for creating the environment
- Enumerate all the procedures required to verify the environment
- Conduct a make or buy analysis (whether to create or buy the environment from outside
- Create your own environment if the environment cannot be acquired from an outside source

Documents to be maintained include anything that supports the fact that the integration environment is available and has been verified.

To that end, you'll want to create a verification checklist:

- Create the procedures and criteria for product integration
- Create procedures to conduct the integration in a planned manner

  - Indicate the number of iterations to be performed
  - Define the integration sequence
  - Specify the level of testing to be conducted
  - Spell out the defined threshold for performance deviation
  - Indicate the interfaces to be verified (e.g., human-machine interfaces, message interfaces, electrical interfaces, or climatic interfaces)
  - Specify the resources required (i.e., testing tools, staff, environment availability, etc.)

Documents to be maintained include the integration procedure (describing your integration criteria). This will help you ensure that your interfaces are compatible. You'll also need to review all interfaces to ensure they are correctly identified and that their coverage is complete.

Documents to be maintained include the review report or record (all identified issues should be closed). Take these steps to manage the interfaces:

- Ensure that interfaces remain compatible with each other for the entire product life cycle
- Resolve any identified issues

Documents to be maintained include those that cover the relationship tables that describe the relationship of product components with each other and the external environment.

Here's an agreed upon list of application program interfaces (APIs) that cover when product components are assembled and delivered:

- Perform checks to determine whether the product components delivered are ready for integration (i.e., a readiness checklist to provide the component acceptance)
- Perform checks to ensure whether integration environment is ready and available

- Assemble the product and product components by following the defined procedures and criteria

- Change/revise the integration procedure if the criteria in the defined procedure does not work

Documents to be maintained include the following:

- A readiness checklist to provide the component acceptance

- Sanity verification/tests

- Created builds

- A revised integration procedure (if required)

You will need to take the following steps to evaluate the assembled product:

- Ensure that the assembled product (e.g., software build, the laptop, and the charger) will work in its intended or end-user environment

- Perform checks/tests to evaluate the assembled product in the end-user environment or in a simulation environment

- Record the test results

- Analyze and correct interface errors, if any

Documents to be maintained include the integration/interface test reports.
Take the following steps to package and deliver the product or product component:

- Once the software build or hardware components are ready, deliver the same to the client as a package (e.g., deliver the software build package in a CD or online file transfer, and provide the hardware package in suitable packaging material)

- Provide the user/client appropriate and sufficient information to take advantage of the delivered material

- Explain what the software build contains (e.g., what modules, patches, and open bugs, if any)

- Provide an installation guide that covers the steps for the user to download and install the delivered software build

- Explain what the hardware package box contains (e.g., servers, laptops, or desktops)

- Provide an installation guide for the user to install the delivered hardware

Documents to be maintained include the following:

- A software build note

- An installation/user guide

- A delivery note that covers software modules, software patches, bugs, hardware, and so on)

- A confirmation receipt for the delivery note

2.3.10.15   Validation

Validation (VAL) is performed along with the client or by the client. The Validation process area covers the following best practices related to preparing for validation:

- Select the product or product components to be validated/tested

  - Product and components include several types of items, like software modules and hardware

  - Technical documents like requirement specifications (i.e., business requirements, software/system requirements, etc.)

  - Design documents (i.e., high and low level)

  - User interfaces (i.e., product integration)

  - User manuals

- Select a validation method for validating the product or product components; there are several possible validation methods

  - A prototype demonstration

  - Tests of products and product components by end users and other relevant stakeholders

  - Formal reviews of technical documents

- Create an environment for performing validation

  - Identify requirements for creating an environment for validation

  - Identify test equipment and tools for performing validation

- Create procedures and criteria for performing validation

  - Create testing procedures

  - Create evaluation procedures

- Perform validation

  - Perform tests on the product or its components as per the defined validation procedure

  - Perform technical documents validation with client

  - Collect validation/test/evaluation results

Documents to be maintained include the following:

- A validation procedure

- Test reports

- Analysis of validation results

- Comparisons of planned vs. actual results

- Analysis of defect data

- Analysis of product or product components which are not working

2.3.10.16   Verification (VER)

Verification is performed internally by the project team members, without involving the client. The Verification process area covers the best practices related to preparing for verification:

- Performing verification requires using various methods
    - Use peer reviews, walkthroughs, simulations, testing, and demonstrations
    - Identify work products to be verified
    - Identify or define a verification method
    - Create an environment for performing verification
    - Identify requirements for creating a verification environment
    - Identify test equipment and tools for performing verification
    - Create procedures and criteria for performing verification
- Performing peer reviews and preparing for peer review
    - Identify members to perform the peer reviews
    - Identify peer review method to be used
    - Create the peer review checklist to be used during the peer review
    - Ensure that entry and exit criteria for the peer review is defined

Documents to be maintained include a peer review checklist.
You can conduct peer reviews using the following methods:

- Review work products and identify defects/other issues
- Document review comments/defects/other issues
- Identify action items resulting from peer reviews
- Communicate action items or any issues to relevant stakeholders
- Ensure that the defined exit criteria for the peer review is met
- If the criteria isn't met, then perform one more round of peer review to meet the exit criteria

Documents to be maintained include a peer review comments/defects report.
The peer review data describes the preparation, conduct, and results. You need to analyze the data in terms of the types of defects:

- Types of defects
- Peer review data analysis report
- Verify selected work products
    - Perform verification of work products (e.g., unit tests and system tests)
    - Record results of verification/tests
    - Identify action items for closure of identified issues

Documents to be maintained include the following:

- Test reports
- Action item log/register

Take these steps to analyze the results of the verification activities:

- Analyze the planned vs. actual result
- Analyze defects data

You'll need to maintain an analysis report with the following information:

- An organizational performance management (OPM)
- An organizational process definition (OPD)
- An organizational process focus (OPF)
- An organizational process performance (OPP)
- An organizational training (OT)

2.3.11 Organizational Process Areas

The third category consists of Organizational process areas; as the term *organization* implies, these process areas contain best practices for the roles to be played by the software engineering process group (SEPG) and the training group in an organization.

2.3.11.1 Organizational Performance Management (OPM)

The Organizational Performance Management (OPM) process area helps you manage business performance and maintain business objectives.

The purpose of OPM is to periodically review and revise the business objectives, along with quality and process performance objectives. It is important to evaluate the business objectives to ensure they are relevant as of today and aligned with the business strategies. For example, you might compare the current business objectives with their actual performance results:

- Ensure that revised business objectives are reviewed and approved by the senior management
- Ensure that revised business objectives are communicated to all

Documents to be maintained include the following:

- A revised business objectives sheet
- A revised quality and process performance objectives sheet
- An analysis of process performance data

On a periodic basis, we need to review the quality and process performance objectives to determine whether the organization is able to meet the current defined business objectives.

For example, if cycle time is one of the critical business objectives, then we need to collect the data from different cycle times and analyze the overall cycle time data with the defined value. If the value matches or is around the defined value, then the organization has the capability to achieve the business objective; otherwise, the organization should revise the business objective value/threshold:

- Identify gaps in the quality and process performance

- Identify if there is any associated risk due to not being able to meet a given business objective

- Communicate the results of process performance and risk analysis to senior management

Documents to be maintained include a report that captures the following:

- Current performance capability vs. defined business objectives

- Identified gaps in process performance

- Identified risks, if any

- Identified potential areas for improvement

- Documented rationale for selecting the improvement area

- Analyzed benefits for implementing the improvement area

You need to communicate to all the relevant stakeholders about implementing the improvement area. In that vein, you'll need to maintain a report that captures the potential areas of improvement:

- Select improvements for implementation

- Elicit improvements from the suggested list (sources could be business objectives, processes, defect causes, etc.)

- Identify improvements as incremental or innovative

  - Incremental improvements are simple and inexpensive to deploy, and may not require rigorous validation (e.g., adding one checkpoint in peer review checklist or a minor update in the tool)

  - Innovative improvements take a more transformational approach to performance improvements

Incremental and innovative improvements are identified by experienced people who have spent a long time in process and technology, or they are identified by a team of experts whose job is to find innovative improvements. These experts can take the following steps:

- Investigate and analyze improvements which may improve process and technologies within the organization

- Perform analysis in terms of improvement benefits (i.e., quantifiable improvement benefits)

- Evaluate the implementation cost, effort, and resources required

- Analyze and document the implementation risks or barriers, if any

- Identify and document the validation method for the deployment of improvements

Documents to be maintained include the following:

- Selected improvement proposals
- Your improvement validation procedure

You must also validate any improvements made:

- Develop a plan for validation (e.g., target projects, a schedule tracker to report results, and measurement activities)
- Review the plan with relevant stakeholders and get agreement on the plan
- Perform validation in an environment similar to the real deployment environment
- Track the validation plan
  - Review and document validation results
  - Must meet the quantitative criteria defined for the improvement

Documents to be maintained include the following:

- A validation plan
- A validation plan tracker
- A validation results report

Once you validate the plan and have a system in place for tracking and reporting on it, you'll need to take steps to select and implement the improvements for deployment:

- Select and prioritize improvement for deployment
- Update the organization process assets

Documents to be maintained include the following:

- Selected improvements deployment list
- Updated organization process documentation

And the next step is to deploy the improvements:

- Plan the deployment for each improvement
- Determine the target population for deployment
- Establish measures and objectives for each deployment to determine the success of the deployment
- Review and agree upon the deployment plan with the stakeholders

Documents to be maintained include a deployment plan for managing development. Follow these steps to monitor your deployment:

- Use training materials to train the people during the deployment
- Ensure that deployment is completed in accordance with the deployment plan
- Document and review deployment results

You will also need to maintain the following documents related to your deployment activities:

- Documented results of deployment activities

- Training material

Finally, you will need to evaluate the effect of your improvements:

- Measure each improvement's defined achievement criteria against the objective

- Measure and analyze the progress of achieving the organization quality and process performance objective

Documents to be maintained include those that measure the effects of each deployment.

2.3.11.2   Organizational Process Definition

The purpose of the Organizational Process Definition (OPD) process area is to define and maintain process assets to be used in the organization by the staff and management. This is also where you define and maintain work environment standards, along with the rules and guidelines for teams.

Follow these steps to establish organizational process assets:

- Establish standard processes

- Define the policies, procedures, templates, guidelines, checklists, and so on to be used in the daily work

- Ensure that critical attributes are present in each process (e.g., the process role, entry criteria, inputs, verification points, outputs, and process and product measures)

- Specify the relationship among process elements (e.g., the order and interface among the process elements)

- Ensure that peer reviews are done on the standard processes

- Revise the standard processes when and as needed (e.g., any improvements are identified in the standard processes)

Documents to be maintained include the following:

- Documented policies

- Procedures

- Templates

- Guidelines

- Checklists

Define and maintain various life-cycle model descriptions

- Select life cycle models based on the project needs of the organization (e.g., waterfall, iterative, spiral, and incremental)

- Describe and document the life-cycle models

- Perform peer review on the life-cycle models

- Revise the life-cycle models when and as needed

Documents to be maintained include documented life-cycle models.

Next, you need to define the tailoring criteria and guidelines:

- Define the criteria and procedure for tailoring the organization standard processes (e.g., modifying a life-cycle model and modifying or replacing process elements)

- Define the process for submission and obtaining the waiver approval from the organizational standard processes

  - Document the tailoring guideline

  - Peer review the tailoring guideline

  - Revise the tailoring guideline when and as needed

Documents to be maintained include the documented tailoring guidelines.

Follow these steps to form the organization measurement repository:

- Identify the organization or senior management needs for storing, retrieving, and analyzing the measurements

- Identify measures which are common for the standard processes (e.g., the work product size, effort and cost, and test coverage)

- Create and update the measurement repository regularly

The measurement repository comprises the following functions:

- Analyze and interpret the measurement data among projects

- Help new projects to quickly identify and access data from the repository by providing meaningful context

- Help improve the accuracy of project estimates by using a project's own historical data (and the historical data of other, similar projects)

- Define procedures for how to store, update, and retrieve measures

- Update the relevant measure's information in the measurement repository

- Ensure that the contents of the measurement repository are available to the relevant/ authorized stakeholders

- At regular intervals, revisit the measurement repository, measures list, and procedures when and as needed

Documents to be maintained include documented and analyzed measurement data.

You will need to form the organizational process asset library. This involves first designing the process asset library, and then deciding which items to be included in the asset library (e.g., policies, procedures, templates, guidelines, checklists, training materials, and lessons learned). Follow these steps:

- Define the criteria for including the items in the library

- Document the procedures for storing, updating, and retrieving the items

- Add the items into the library and list them for easy access by the project and various other teams

- On a periodic basis, review the use of each item

Documents to be maintained include a documented process asset–master list (i.e., a list of items in the process asset library).

Follow these steps to define the work-environment standards:

- Identify and follow the work-environment standards that are appropriate for use in the organization

- Revise the work environment-standards on a periodic basis and fill the gaps wherever necessary

Documents to be maintained include documented work-environment standards.

Following these steps will help you establish rules and guidelines for teams:

- For timely decision making, empower the teams by documenting and deploying organizational guidelines

- Define the rules and guidelines for structuring and forming teams

- Define the rules and guidelines for how teams will work in a collective manner (e.g., how the work will be accomplished, who will perform reviews and approve the work, and how the resources and inputs will be accessed)

Documents to be maintained include documented rules and guidelines for your teams.

2.3.11.3   Organizational Process Focus

The Organizational Process Focus process area (OPF) enables you to plan, implement, and deploy organizational process improvements by following these steps:

- Determine process improvement opportunities

- Determine strengths, weaknesses, and improvement opportunities by following a standard or model (i.e., the ISO 9001 or CMMI model)

- Establish organizational process needs

  - Identify and examine the process model or standards that are applicable to the organization (e.g., CMMI or ISO 9001)

  - Document the organization's process needs and objectives

Documents to be maintained include those that document the organization's process needs and objectives.

Here is how you appraise the organization's processes:

- Perform appraisals to identify processes which need improvement and to satisfy the needs of a customer-supplier relationship

- Obtain buy-in from the senior management for the appraisal sponsorship

- Define the scope of the appraisal (e.g., a single business unit, a site, or the whole organization) for selected projects and functions

- Determine the method for the process appraisal (i.e., the appraisal method is different for CMMI and ISO 9001, so it's necessary to know the need of each appraisal type)

    - Plan, schedule, and conduct the process appraisal

    - Document and deliver the appraisal results or findings

Documents to be maintained include the following:

- A plan for organization process appraisal

- An appraisal for findings results/recommendations

At this stage, you need to identify the organization's process improvements:

- Determine the improvements for the candidate process

- Review and use appropriate techniques to identify candidate process improvements

    - Customer satisfaction survey results

    - Processes

    - Lessons learned from implementing processes using inputs from senior management and by conducting the process appraisals

- Prioritize the candidate process improvements

    - Perform the cost-benefit analysis

    - Identify and document each process improvement with a priority

Documents to be maintained include those that document the process improvements to be implemented. The next step is to plan and implement your process actions; here's how you define process actions plans:

- Process improvements to be addressed

- Process improvement infrastructure

- Process improvement objectives

    - Any piloting that needs to be done

    - Resources and schedules

    - Any identified risks to be tracked

- Set the process action teams to implement actions

Documents to be maintained include those related to your approved process action plans. Follow these steps to implement process actions plans:

- Negotiate and document commitments among the process action teams

- Track progress and commitments, and conduct joint reviews with the relevant stakeholders

- Plan pilots, if needed

- Identify and track issues to closure

- Ensure that the implemented process-improvement plan has resulted in the achievement of the process-improvement objectives

You will need to maintain the following documents:

- The documented commitment of the process action teams
- A progress report for the improvement plan

Follow these steps to create plans for pilots:

- Deploy organizational process assets and incorporate appropriate experiences
- Deploy organizational process assets throughout the organization or the business unit
    - Identify how organizational process assets will be made available to the teams (e.g., via a web site)
    - Ensure that process training is delivered to all the teams
    - Identifying how changes to organizational-process assets are communicated
- Deploy standard processes
    - Identify projects in the organization which are starting up
    - Identify current active projects which could benefit from the deployment of standard processes
    - Set the plans to implement the deployment of standard processes
    - Assist projects in identifying and adapting the tailoring on the standard processes
    - Maintain the tailoring records
    - Whenever standard processes are improved, identify the projects which should implement the changes as per the improved processes

Documents to be maintained include the following:

- The organization's list of projects and the status of process deployment for each
- Guidelines to deploy the standard processes on new projects
- Tailoring records

Once you decide how to deploy your process assets, you will need to monitor the implementation:

- Monitor projects in which standard processes are deployed
- Review process artifacts created during the life of each project to ensure that all projects are making appropriate use of the organization's set of standard processes
- Conduct process compliance checks to gauge how well standard processes have been deployed
- Identify and track any deployment issues to closure

Documents to be maintained include the following:

- Reports of process implementation monitoring on projects
- Process compliance audit reports
- Results of reviews of selected process artifacts; these get created as part of process tailoring and implementation

Next, you'll need to follow these steps to incorporate experiences into the organizational process assets:

- Conduct periodic reviews to check the effectiveness and suitability of the organization's set of standard processes

- Obtain feedback from the staff members of the organization who are using the standard processes

- Identify the lessons learned when defining, piloting, implementing, and deploying organizational processes

- Analyze measurement data obtained by using the common set of measures

- Appraise processes, methods, and tools to develop recommendations for improving organizational process

- Establish and maintain records of the process-improvement activities conducted across the organization

Documents to be maintained include the following:

- Process-improvement proposals

- Process lessons learned

- Records of the organization's process-improvement activities

2.3.11.4   Organizational Process Performance (OPP)

The Organizational Process Performance (OPP) process area defines organizational quantitative objectives and establishes the process performance baseline and models to quantitatively manage the projects.
Follow these steps to establish performance baselines and models:

- Define the quantitative objectives for quality and process performance at the organizational level

- Set quantitative objectives for process and subprocess measurements (e.g., effort, cycle time, and defect density)

Documents to be maintained include those related to the organization's quality and process performance objectives.
Actually selecting processes or subprocesses requires following these steps:

- Define the criteria for the selection of a process or subprocess, including examples like the following:

  - The process or subprocess is strongly related to key business objectives

  - The availability of historical data is relevant to the process or subprocess

  - The process or subprocess will generate data to enable statistical management

- Select the subprocesses and document the rationale for their selection

- Establish and maintain traceability between the selected subprocesses, quality and process performance objectives, and business objectives, including examples like the following:

  - Subprocess mapping with quality and process performance objectives

  - Subprocess mapping with the business objectives

Documents to be maintained include a list of processes or subprocesses identified for process-performance analyses.

Follow these steps to establish process-performance measures:

- Establish measures for both product and process attributes, based on the selected process or subprocess

- Possible criteria for selecting such measures can include the following:

    - The relationship of measures to the organization's quality and process performance objectives

    - Coverage that measures provide over the life of the product or service

    - The frequency at which observations of measures can be collected

- The operational definitions for the selected measures from the organization's set of common measures

2.3.11.5   Establish Process Performance Models

Process-performance models can help an organization to estimate or predict the value of a process-performance measure. Projects can use them for estimating, analyzing, and predicting the process performance of their defined processes.

Examples of process-performance models include the following:

- Regression models

- Monte Carlo simulation models

You can create process performance models by referring to the organization's standard processes and process performance baselines. Follow these steps to do so:

- Review process-performance models with relevant stakeholders and get their agreement on the same

- Revise process-performance models whenever required (e.g., when processes are improved/updated)

Documents to be maintained include the process-performance models.

2.3.11.6   Organizational Training

The purpose of the Organizational Training (OT) process area is to provide skills and enhance the knowledge of the staff, in order to help them perform their roles in an efficient manner. Follow these steps to establish an organizational training capability, which will help ensure that the organization's strategic training needs are identified.

Sources of strategic training needs include the following:

- An organization's standard processes

- An organization's strategic business plan

- An organization's process improvement plan

You will also need to perform regular skill assessments. Categories of training needs include the following:

- Engineering (e.g., requirements analysis, design, testing, configuration management, and quality assurance)

- Team building

- Leadership

One of the most important aspects of training a staff is to perform ongoing needs analysis:

- Identify which training which will be the responsibility of the organization and which will be left to the individual project or support group

- Analyze and negotiate how training needs identified by projects and support groups will be met

- Document commitments from the staff for providing training support to projects and support groups

You need to maintain documents that cover common project and support group training needs. Outlining training commitments involves creating and maintaining an annual training plan. Setting the content of the plan includes spelling out the following:

- Training topics

- Methods used for training

- Training tasks

- Roles and responsibilities

- Schedules based on training activities

- Required resources (e.g., tools, facilities, environments, staffing, skills, and knowledge)

You'll need to document the commitments from those who are responsible for implementing and supporting the plan, and then revisit the plan and documented commitments whenever necessary.

You'll need to maintain an annual training plan for the organization.

2.3.11.7 Establish a Training Capability

You'll need to select the appropriate method to satisfy organizational training needs. Examples of possible training approaches include the following:

- Classroom training

- Self-study

- Formal apprenticeship

- Mentoring programs

- Structured on-the-job training

Following these steps will also help you to establish an appropriate training plan:

- Assess the need to develop training materials internally or to acquire them externally

- Develop or obtain qualified instructors or mentors

- Maintain the training calendar (e.g., topics to be covered, training objectives, and intended audience)

- Revise training materials and supporting artifacts, as necessary

Documents to be maintained include your training materials and supporting artifacts. Follow these steps to provide training for your organization:

- Identify those staff members who need to attend trainings and are necessary to execute their roles effectively

- Schedule trainings, including any resources, as necessary (e.g., facilities and instructors)

- Track the training delivery against the plan

Documents to be maintained include the delivered training course. You'll need to establish and maintain records of your organizational training, including the following:

- Keep records of participants who successfully completed training courses, as well as those who were unsuccessful

- Keep records of all staff waiver requests

- Make training records available to the appropriate people

Documents to be maintained include the training records. You'll need to assess the effectiveness of the organization's training program and build a mechanism to assess the effectiveness of each training course, as per the defined objectives. Here are some methods you can use to assess training effectiveness:

- The post-training feedback of participants

- Surveys of manager satisfaction, including ratings

- Assessment through courseware provided

Documents to be maintained include the following:

- Training effectiveness surveys

- Instructor evaluation forms

- Training examinations

2.3.12   Support Process Areas

The fourth category is comprised of Support process areas. As the term implies, these process areas contain best practices for the roles to be played by the project manager, configuration manager/controller, technical/functional Leads, and the SQA/auditor in an organization.

2.3.12.1   Causal Analysis and Resolution

The Causal Analysis and Resolution process area helps you analyze causes and problems in both negative and positive ways. If there is a negative impact, this process area can help you prevent the causes or problems from reoccurring.

If a cause has a positive impact, this process area can help you incorporate the cause into processes in a way that contributes to more successful outcomes in your organization. This will help in improving/repeating the performance of the process.

To begin, you need to figure out the causes of selected outcomes. You might be wondering why you are interested only in selected outcomes. This is because not all outcomes have an equal impact, and only some impacts require an action.

The next step is to select outcomes for performing the analysis. We can initiate/plan analysis in two ways:

1.   Trigger an event

2.   Execute a periodic/planned activity at the beginning of a phase or task

You'll need to gather data for analysis (real time/current data would be best for this analysis). Types of data to gather for this include the following:

- Customer or end user reported defects

- Peer review comments/defects

- Test defects

- Process capability problems

- Customer feedback points/low ratings

After the selecting the type of data to analyze, you need to select the outcomes to analyze further. Methods which could be used to select outcomes include the following:

- Pareto analysis

- Histograms

During the selection of outcomes, focus on their source, impact, frequency of occurrence, the cost of performing the analysis, the required time and resources needed, and so on.

Also, clearly define the scope of analysis, improvement expected, the stakeholders that will be affected, and so on.

At this point, you're ready to analyze the causes:

- Perform root cause analysis with members who are responsible for performing the task

- Identify root causes using appropriate methods

    - Cause and effect (fishbone) diagram

    - Check sheets

- Group the causes based on their identified root causes

    - Inadequate training and skills

    - Making mistakes in procedures

- Create an action plan

    - Address negative causes and prevent them from reoccurring

    - Incorporate best practices into the processes

Examples of preventive actions include the following:

- Training

- Tools

- Methods

Examples of best practices include the following:

- Create an activity checklist to avoid common problems

- Update the process to remove error-prone steps

- Automate part or all of a process

Documents to be maintained include an action plan. This means you'll need to analyze and select an action plan for implementation.

It is important to analyze and select a variety of factors are when implementing your plan. Factors to analyze might include timelines, cost, stakeholders involved, benefits expected, and so on.

Implement an action plan to accomplish the following:

- Track the plan (i.e. tasks, people, etc.)

- Review results

- Track action items to closure

Let's walk through what an improvement action plan might look like when using a new tool. Following these steps will help you evaluate the effect of implemented actions:

- Measure and analyze the change in performance of affected processes

- Review the before and after analysis of the performance

- Determine whether the change in performance has brought a positive impact (i.e., does it help you meet project quality and process performance objectives?)

- Plan an appropriate action if the change in performance does not help you achieve the expected project quality benefits

Documents to be maintained include the following:

- An updated plan

- An updated action item log/register

- A before-and-after process performance analysis report

Be sure to record your causal analysis data:

- The purpose of this is to make the data available to other projects, so that they can use/refer to the data in order to achieve similar results

- Once the implemented action plan is found to be effective, submit the information to the organization for inclusion in the organizational processes

Documents to be maintained include the following:

- Causal analysis data

- An improvement proposal

2.3.12.2   Configuration Management

The Configuration Management (CM) process area helps you accomplish several tasks:

- Identify configurable items

- Perform configuration control

- Maintain the integrity of baselines

- Maintain configuration status accounting

- Conduct configuration audits

- Establish baselines for work products

- Identify configurable items

    - Configuration items could be hardware and equipment, as well as software and documentation

    - The criteria for selecting a configurable item are based on whether a work product is expected to change over time (e.g., is there a change in the requirements?)

Examples of configurable items include the following:

- A requirement specification

- Design

- Source code

- Test plans and procedures

- Tools

For each configurable item, assign a unique identification mark (e.g., Design_<client name>_1.0.doc). You'll need to decide when to place each configuration item under a configuration management. Here are some examples:

- Work product test readiness

- A project-lifecycle phase

- The degree of control analyzed on each work product

- An owner assigned for each configuration item

Documents to be maintained include a configuration-management plan.

2.3.12.3   Create a Configuration-Management System

You'll need to manage multiple levels of control for the work product. Examples of this include the following:

- *Uncontrolled*: Changes can be done by any staff member

- *Work in progress*: The author is controlling the changes

- *Released*: Changes are controlled by authorized personnel only; when any changes are made, the relevant stakeholders are updated

Following these steps will help you build an effective configuration-management system:

- Manage access control for each project member; the goal is to ensure that only authorized people have access to the relevant project folders or configuration management system (i.e., CVS, VSS, etc.)

- Store, update, and retrieve configuration management records

- Create release baselines for internal use, as well as for delivery to the customer

  - A software baseline might include requirements, design, source code files, build files, and user documentation

- Obtain approval from the change control board (CCB) for the creation and release of baselines for configuration items

- Track the configuration items which are in a baseline state

You will also need to track and control changes:

- Track change requests for configuration items

- Track the change requests received in a change request tracker sheet/tool

- Perform impact analysis based on the received change request

- Set the priority for each received change request

- Review change requests in the CCB meeting and get approval from relevant stakeholders

- Track the status of each change request until closure

You will also need to track change requests for configuration items:

- For each configuration item, control the changes throughout the project or service life cycle

- Obtain approval from CCB members before updating a configuration item and placing it in the configuration management system

- All check in and check out should be done properly, without losing the previous versions

- Document the reasons for making the changes to a configuration item

- Following these steps will help you establish the integrity of a baseline:

- Ensure that each configuration item status is known, and that recovery of previous versions is possible

- Ensure that relevant stakeholders are aware of the configuration status of configuration items

- Ensure that the difference between the previous and the current baseline is known

- Ensure that you are using the latest version of the baseline

Documents to be maintained include the following:

- A change log

- Change requests

You can track configuration status by performing configuration audits:

- Check and ensure that configuration items are complete and correct in the configuration-management system

- Check and ensure that configuration management standards and procedures are followed

- Ensure that all configuration audit findings are closed

Documents to be maintained include a configuration audit report that shows the status of your findings.

2.3.12.4   Decision Analysis and Resolution

The Decision Analysis and Resolution (DAR) process area enables us to analyze possible decisions during the project by using formal evaluation techniques/methods. The evaluation method will help us evaluate the alternatives identified, and then complete the process by choosing the best alternative available. We will need to do the following:

- Evaluate alternatives

- Create guidelines for decision-making analysis

Creating the guidelines is important, as it will help us to decide which decisions need to be evaluated using the formal evaluation technique/method. Only some decisions require evaluation because not every decision is significant enough to be evaluated through the formal evaluation process.

Here are some sample points that might be mentioned in the guidelines; these can help in determining which decisions to be put under the formal evaluation process:

- Issues which can lead to medium- to high-impact risk

- Decisions required for changing the work products placed under configuration management

- Decisions which could lead to delays over a certain amount of time

- Decisions which can affect achieving the objectives of the project

Here are some activities for which the formal evaluation process could be used:

- To procure material

- To design alternative decisions

- To make decisions on the cycle time or response time of a process

Documents to be maintained include a guideline document, which covers when to use the formal evaluation process.

2.3.12.5   Establish Evaluation Criteria

The guideline document is the basis for evaluating alternative solutions. Each defined criteria will be given a ranking, and the highest ranked criteria get more weight in the selection process:

- Define the criteria for evaluating alternative solutions

- Rank the criteria and define the range and scale

- Rank and assess each selected criterion during the evaluation

- Document the rationale/reasons for choosing the selected criteria

Documents to be maintained include a guideline document that covers the criteria, with rankings that you can use to identify alternative solutions.

You can search the alternative solutions both within and outside the organization. Within the organization, you can determine whether any other business unit or department has already worked on the solution. And outside the organization, you can determine if you can procure a ready-made solution which can be plugged into the existing, running system. Brainstorm with a technical and/or experienced member of your teams to identify suitable alternatives:

- Document the final alternatives list

- Select from among the several evaluation methods

    - Surveys

    - Engineering studies

    - Field experience and prototypes

    - Expert judgment (i.e., the Delphi method)

Also, measures need to be identified to support the evaluation method (e.g., the impact on cost, schedule, performance, and risk).

Choose the evaluation method which is most relevant to support the evaluation process:

- Evaluate alternative solutions

- Evaluate alternatives based on the defined criteria and the selected evaluation method

- Evaluate uncertainty in the values for alternative solutions (e.g., if the score varies between two values, then you need to assess whether there is a significant difference and whether it will affect the selection of the final solution)

- Address the uncertainty by taking appropriate actions

    - Perform simulations

    - Build prototypes

    - Run pilots

- Select the best solution from the alternatives evaluated

    - Assess the risk, if any, associated with the solution selected from the alternatives

    - Document the rationale for selecting the final solution and communicate the results to the relevant stakeholders

2.3.12.6   Measurement and Analysis

The purpose of the Measurement and Analysis (MA) process area is to establish a measurement system in the organization or the software unit group of the organization. The measurement system will help in measuring and assessing the project objectives, which in turn will help in achieving the business/ organization objective.

Follow these steps to align the measurement and analysis activities:

- Establish the measurement objectives

- Document the measurement objectives

The measurement objectives enable you to perform measurement and analysis activities in the organization. Sources for the information needs and objectives can include the following:

- Project plans

- Business plans

- Interviews with managers

- Industry benchmarks

- Experience of other objects in the organization

You will want to review and update measurement objectives with management and other relevant stakeholders.

Documents to be maintained include your measurement objectives, which specify your organization's measures.

Here, measurement objectives are converted into quantifiable measures. Examples of measures include the following:

- Effort variance

- Schedule variance

- Defect density

- Defects measure (i.e., the number of defects by severity and the total number of defects)

- Customer satisfaction ratings and trends

You will also need to document the operational definitions of measures. For example, you will need to state what to measure, how to measure it, the unit of measurement for each measure, as well as what has been included or excluded. Be sure to prioritize, review, and update measures with the relevant end users and stakeholders.

Documents to be maintained include the measurement guidelines. In these guidelines, you specify the process, including how measurement data will be obtained and stored:

- Identify measures for which existing sources of data are available

- Identify those measures for which data is needed, but which is currently not available

- Identify for each measure how to collect and store that data

- Work on the data-collection mechanism and procedures

- Update the measures and measurement objectives, as needed

You will also need to specify how measurement data is analyzed and communicated:

- Identify each type of data analysis to be conducted and the reports to be generated

- Select the appropriate data analysis methods and tools

    - Pie charts

    - Bar charts

    - Histograms

    - Line charts

- Review the measurement report with relevant stakeholders, end users, data providers, and so on

- Define the criteria for evaluating the measurement analysis results (e.g., determine whether the data is reliable, understandable, and can be used for decision making)

You will use the measurement guidelines to accomplish the following:

- Provide measurement results

    - Collect measurement data

    - Perform data calculations

    - Perform data integrity checks (i.e., errors in data, unusual patterns, etc.)

- Analyze measurement data

    - Perform analysis and interpret results to draw conclusions

    - Review the results with the relevant stakeholders before releasing it to all the stakeholders

    - Refine the measurement process based on the lessons learned during the reviews

Documents to be maintained include a draft of the measurement reports.
You will want to follow these guidelines to store data and results:

- Store data as per the defined data-storage procedures

- Ensure data is available to only authorized groups

- Prevent information from being used inappropriately

Documents to be maintained include the measurement data inventory.
Follow these steps to communicate the results:

- In a timely manner, regularly update the relevant stakeholders about the measurement results

- Help the relevant stakeholders to understand the results

Documents to be maintained include the measurement analysis report; this report needs to include read me guidelines for understanding the report.

2.3.12.7   Process and Product Quality Assurance (PPQA)

The Process and Product Quality Assurance (PPQA) process area helps you to accomplish the following:

- Objectively evaluate the process actions and work products against the defined processes and standards in the organization QMS

- Identify process noncompliance issues

- Communicate feedback to project teams on the quality assurance activities

- Ensure that the process noncompliance issues are closed

Examples of objective evaluations include the following:

- Internal quality audits conducted by the audit group

- A review of work products

- Performance reviews at the work places (i.e., desk audits)

These steps can help you objectively evaluate processes:

- Define clear criteria for evaluating the processes

- Evaluate the selected processes

- Identify noncompliance issues

- Identify lessons learned for process improvement

Follow these steps to objectively evaluate work products:

- Define clear criteria for evaluating the work products

- Evaluate the selected work products based on the sampling criteria

- Identify noncompliance issues

- Identify the lessons learned for process improvement

Documents to be maintained include the following:

- Evaluation reports

- Quality assurance reports

Follow these steps to track noncompliance issues and ensure resolution:

- Resolve the noncompliance issue with the relevant project members

- Document the noncompliance issues when they are not resolved in the project

- Escalate to senior management when noncompliance issues are not resolved in the project, so that appropriate actions can be taken

- Analyze noncompliance issues to see whether there are any formation trends regarding a particular category, so that appropriate action can be taken

- Ensure that you communicate the evaluation results to relevant stakeholders

You will also want to establish and maintain records of the quality-assurance activities:

- Document the result and status of quality-assurance activities performed
- Revise the status of quality-assurance activities performed

Documents to be maintained include the following:

- Quality-assurance reports
- Status reports

Hopefully we have covered all the process areas and their mapping. Although space prohibits explaining every point in-depth, we hope you will find the material in this chapter easy-to-follow and simple-to-understand.

2.4   Summary

In this chapter, we have learned about the structure of the CMMI and how to interpret the structure. We have also covered 22 process areas. Most of the information and pointers in this chapter are taken from the CMMI model. The model information is very vast, but we have tried to explain purpose of various process areas in a simple, straightforward, and easy-to-understand manner.

CHAPTER 3

■ ■ ■

Planning CMMI Implementation

In this chapter, we will discuss CMMI implementation, with a special emphasis on how to initiate, plan, and start a CMMI implementation.

3.1 Initiating CMMI Implementation

Since you are now planning to initiate a CMMI implementation, you should ask yourself, "Do I need CMMI?"

As a first step, we need to understand what we want to achieve and deliver as part of our product development or service delivery. As for improving the process maturity, we need to consider what results are expected. It's only by considering issues in this way that we can answer why we need CMMI.

If CMMI is not the solution for your problem, then you need to analyze what can work better for you and your organization. Many organizations want to implement CMMI to meet the project's bidding criteria or perhaps because the client wants to work with only CMMI Appraised companies. To meet such scenarios, an organization will only get maturity level; however, it won't be considered a matured organization in terms of its processes.

3.1.1 Understand Your Business

Here are few questions which could help you understand your business needs and move you towards the CMMI implementation:

- What products or services are offered by your organization?

- How many business units do you have, and do all of them produce the same or similar products/services?

- Have you identified key business units for you to succeed?

- Is there any scope for improvement? And which part of the business process do you want to improve?

- What is the current cycle time of your services or products?

- What is the current resource competency that you have?

- Are your clients expecting certain maturity in some processes?

Whenever you want to bring a vast change into your business process, or you want to introduce new process, it will always take some time as most people will have differences of opinion on how to proceed. Hence, an internal discussion within management and key decision makers about what CMMI is—and what kinds of benefits can be expected from implementing the model—will help reduce anxiety in the minds of stakeholders.

© Mukund Chaudhary 2017
M. Chaudhary and A. Chopra, *CMMI for Development*, DOI 10.1007/978-1-4842-2529-5_3

To start an implementation, organization and implementation teams can initially focus on one business unit and slowly move on to other business units. This is the option for those organizations that are not yet ready to cover the whole organization, and would prefer to start with one business unit at a time. This makes sense in a way because to include new process changes requires time and involvement; organizations see this is as a big challenge to implement while simultaneously delivering projects to their clients as part of running the business.

3.1.2   Engage CMMI Institute Partner

With the help of CMMI institute web site, you can easily find provider within your region. To search a provider, go to http://partners.cmmiinstitute.com/find-partner-organization/.

Next, select your partner of choice from the list or use the advanced search option to select the product suite, and then to select the geographic location for your search. Figure 3-1 shows the search screen from CMMI Institute web site.

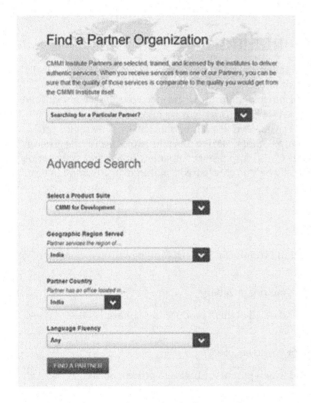

Figure 3-1.   *The search screen to find a provider*

You should discuss the following points with the consulting partner (these points must also be understood by the subject matter expert team members):

- The current version of CMMI model

- Implementation steps

- Experience in similar implementations

- Goals and objectives to be achieved

- Resource requirements (e.g., human, infrastructure, and training requirements)

- The right constellation to be adopted

- You need to discuss how long it typically takes to

- You also need to discuss how long it typically takes to implement the CMMI model in an organization like yours, as well as the maturity level you should target.

■ **Note**   We have to enroll authorized CMMI partners for the appraisal services; however, there are no such restrictions for consulting or SME services.

3.1.3   Choosing the Right Constellation

Choosing a constellation for implementing CMMI is important; choosing the right one for the business to benefit is more even important. (We have already covered constellations in Chapter 2). It's also possible to take the advice of our consulting partner for choosing the right constellation. We also recommend examining a few factors when choosing a constellation:

- The business model in the organization

- The product delivery cycle time

- The complexities involved in product development

- Areas where more improvement is required

There could be additional factors that influence your decision. However, the best practice says that, when you have smaller cycle times with less intensive engineering needs to deliver the product or services, then it is recommended that you go for CMMI Services. However, if your business model delivers both product development and services (i.e., maintenance, migration, testing, etc.), then it is recommended that you go with combined CMMI Dev and CMMI Svc Constellations to implement the best from both. Please discuss these options your CMMI Partner.

However, if you are delivering projects with durations ranging from shorter (three to nine months) or longer projects (more than nine months), and it is expected that you maintain good process delivery practices, then it is recommended that you implement the CMMI Dev model.

■ **Tip**   CMMI for Services (SVC) also contains engineering practices for the Service System Development process area.

3.1.4   Engaging a CMMI Institute Partner or Service Provider

We have already discussed that you need to engage a CMMI Institute partner (i.e., CMMI Institute Certified Individuals or consulting services provider) for performing the following:

- Official CMMI training

- Consulting/guidance in CMMI implementation

- Appraisal activity

CMMI implementation guidance can be carried out by SMEs available within the organization or a consulting partner hired from outside the organization; no certification is required for the SMEs to provide guidance or consultancy for any organization.

It is only if you want to achieve a maturity level rating for your organization processes that it becomes mandatory to use a CMMI Institute certified lead appraiser for performing the appraisal.

Lead appraiser services can be acquired through a CMMI Institute Partner. It is always a best practice to engage a lead appraiser early in your implementation if you have plan for CMMI Implementation with appraisal; doing so will help ensure the lead appraiser's availability for the month in which your organization has decided to conduct CMMI appraisal. (A lead appraiser can perform only two appraisals in a month).

Selection of a Lead Appraiser is very important, and you must consider or list a few points before selecting a lead appraiser for your maturity ratings:

- Consider the overall experience of a lead appraiser

- Check the lead appraiser's credibility in the IT industry

- Investigate past experience in conducting CMMI appraisals for organizations similar to your own

- Be sure to check the lead appraiser CMMI appraisal calendar, as sometimes you may not get lead appraiser dates for the month in which your organization is planning to conduct the final appraisal. There is a cap of two appraisals per month, so it is important to understand whether the lead appraiser is available for your desired timeframe.

These are also some of the generic points to consider before engaging any lead appraiser.

If an organization is only focusing on implementation of CMMI—and it neither wants to conduct an appraisal nor is looking for a process rating in the near future—then the services of a CMMI partner or lead appraiser won't especially be needed.

■ **Note**   A lead appraiser cannot be a consultant for you; and if you have your own lead appraiser in your organization, then that person can't appraise your organization.

3.2   Identify and Form Teams

Once you are convinced and are ready for a CMMI implementation, the first thing you need to do is identify and form a subject matter expert team. The purpose of forming this team is to drive CMMI implementation within your organization across the business units.

This team's existence is important as, during the implementation, there will be various stages where important decisions need to be made; and at that time, this team will have an important role to play in the areas they will be responsible for. You will learn more about this role later in this chapter and the book.

Who should be the part of subject matter expert team, and where do you find its members? Mostly, you find them in mid- to large-size organizations. Typically, it is the quality head from the SQA group (not testing) or the process quality group who drives the CMMI implementation, with the nod of Senior Management. But, if you don't have this group currently running in your organization, then it is advisable that you hire the quality head and create the SQA group.

A quality head would have the required quality management system (QMS) formation and the management background. The CMMI model puts its emphasis mainly on improving organization QMS, which consists of your processes. The quality head/SQA group would act as an unbiased, independent, separate entity within the organization. This group will be a big help for the engineering/delivery teams in writing the processes because people from an engineering background are typically not fond of process writing—yes, that is a surprising fact.

■ **Note**   The previously mentioned point about hiring and forming a quality head/SQA group is only advice. Organizations still can manage implementation without this group, as members from engineering/delivery teams could also play this role. The only difference is that members from the engineering/delivery teams have to put in more effort during the implementation exercise, along with their project delivery role.

Organizations which are small and are not very keen to form an SQA group, can contact any CMMI Partners in your region who are providing Consulting and Appraisal services. These partners will help and guide you in your CMMI implementation journey in every possible manner.

3.3   Decide Roles and Responsibilities

The quality head/group will drive and help in the identification and formation of teams, along with assigning their roles and responsibilities. It's important to form the teams early because, once an organization takes the decision to implement CMMI, staff members have to be involved from various groups/departments/business units. These staff members have to be chosen carefully for the implementation; hence, members with relevant experience and knowledge should be approached to form a team.

Also, the time availability of these staff members is a key factor during the implementation. We need to assess how much time they will be able to spend apart from their day-to-day project/product delivery tasks. This is important because CMMI implementation activities for an organization may take six to seven months until final appraisal on average; and for some organizations, this time period is very crucial because implementation is linked with the organization's business objective to be achieved in a year or two. Hence, the time commitment from the key members is very important. If they are not available for any crucial project/product delivery or any other business reason, then the CMMI implementation activities/schedule might get delayed in completion.

Next, we'll look at a typical team formation for a CMMI Implementation.

3.3.1   CMMI Program/Project Manager

As the name suggests, a CMMI program/project manager is responsible for monitoring and controlling the CMMI journey in your organization. Note that it is not mandatory to have full time person for this role. Any senior person within the organization can be dedicated or partially allocated for this role. Here are a few of this person's responsibilities:

- CMMI program planning and monitoring

- Manages stakeholders' commitment

- Status reporting to senior management

- Participates in SEPG meetings

- Helps in achieving plans

- Performs risk management

Looking at these responsibilities, you can see the similarities to the way a program manager manages products or services.

3.3.2   Software Engineering Process Group (SEPG)

A software engineering process group is a group of subject matter experts (SMEs) from an engineering or management background, along with process quality assurance members from within an organization. This group will be responsible for owning and running software process improvement activities.

A few of the SMEs can work as permanent members of the group, and others can work on an as needed basis. Here are some of the responsibilities played by the SEPG, which is sometimes called an Engineering Process Group (EPG):

- Ensures that relevant processes are defined and aligned with business objectives to support the delivery of product or services

- Ensures that process assets are revised and maintained on a regular basis, based on identified improvements

- Reviews and approves process tailoring

- Ensures that processes are appraised from time-to-time, in order to assess the strengths and weaknesses of current processes

If your organization aims to implement and achieve maturity level 4 and maturity level 5, then organizational performance management (OPM) also will be owned by SEPG.

3.3.3   PQA or SQA Group

A process quality assurance (PQA) or software quality assurance (SQA) group consists of people who have good knowledge of the process quality assurance or the software quality assurance.

■ **Note**   PQA and SQA members are *not* part of the software testing group; as per CMMI, QA is part of testing and peer reviews, which is called verification and is performed by the project team. QC is done at the client end, which is validation.

The typical responsibilities of this group include, but are not limited to, the following:

- Project reviews/audits

- Deliver process trainings

- Product and process quality reviews

- Process compliance checks

- Project metrics collation and analysis

- Providing relevant process improvement updates to SEPG

3.3.4   Metrics Analyst Group

The metrics analyst group is a subgroup of the SEPG group. These are SMEs who collect and analyze/understand project metrics data. The analysis of project metrics data needs to be meaningful for the project and organization to use it for informed decision making.

This group generally does not exist in most of organizations, and some organizations combine their project management office with metrics group.

Typical responsibilities of the metrics analyst group include the following:

- Metrics data collection from projects on a monthly basis

- Perform metrics analysis

- Use analysis to identify and baseline new metrics

3.3.5   Training Group

The training group in an organization can work as the separate/independent group, or it can work in combination with the Human Resource (HR) group. This group's main role is to do the following:

- Identify the training needs in the organization

- Plan and conduct Trainings

- Assess training effectiveness

- Improve the training delivery process

So far, we've covered the composition of teams and their formation with a clear understanding of their roles and responsibilities. Now it's to schedule the CMMI Implementation activities.

If you think from the perspective of a program manager or project manager, you know the value of effort estimation. Each task involved in the program should be estimated, and you should be able to schedule activities that fit within your target.

Hence, you need to be clear that it is not only a project for your organization, but that it is also for cultural change within your organization, which may take some time to show the results.

If you or senior management decides to implement CMMI practices within your organization, then please do check and assess whether you have sufficient time available to achieve the target.

3.4   Plan CMMI Implementation and Activities

Before we move ahead to planning phase of CMMI, we should draw our attention to some of the common reasons which could make our CMMI Implementation ineffective.

The reasons for an ineffective implementation might include the following:

- No participation from management

- CMMI Implementation only for the client needs

- Lack of project management skills

- Resistance to change

- No process improvement expectation setting

The SME team has to note the first important step is to plan and conduct the gap analysis with respect to the current method/process/practice followed for product and/or service delivery. This means it is necessary to know and understand where the gaps are before we start filling them; in other words, we must know the right areas that need focus and improvement. Identifying more gaps during the gap analysis exercises will help us make the organization processes more robust.

This would help in planning the activities, creating timelines, estimating resources, and devising strategies for effective implementation of CMMI. Hence, gap analysis is the first recommended step in planning.

3.4.1   Process Gap Analysis

By definition, gap analysis is the process of comparing the actual performance with the potential or desired performance. Gap analysis is the formal study of what a business is currently doing and how its processes are defined and followed; and then determining whether these processes are helping the organization to reach the goals it wants to achieve in the future. Gap analysis can be done from different perspectives, such as resource availability, business processes, and information technology.

Performing gap analysis involves studying artifacts and interviewing or discussing these issues with the practitioners. These interviews are mostly conducted with the project manager and the program manager who are involved in the service/delivery of products/project.

3.4.2   How Gap Analysis Is Conducted

Let examine how gap analysis is conducted.

Gap analysis will be performed with the CMMI partner selected by you for CMMI implementation and appraisal services.

A CMMI partner cum external consultant will review the plan and meet the teams that we have discussed creating so far in this chapter.

It's possible that certain teams won't yet exist at the time of scheduling the process gap analysis (e.g., the SEPG group or Metrics Analyst Group might not exist yet), and this can be assumed to be part of the known gap. Obviously, interviewing non-existent teams during the gap analysis exercises is not possible.

During the gap analysis, the external consultant will interview people from the following existing teams:

- Project/Program delivery managers

- SEPG/Metrics Analyst Group

- SQA/Quality Group

- Training Group

The external consultant will also review the existing processes/artifacts:

- He will review processes for project management, engineering, and support

- He will review artifacts created as part of the project, such as the project plan, the requirement document, the design, and so on

The consultant's basis for interviewing and reviewing processes/artifacts is the CMMI Dev model, including the following components in particular:

> Process areas
>
> Generic goals
>
> Generic practices
>
> Specific goals
>
> Specific practices

If any gap is noted/reported by the external consultant, it means that either one or more of the previously mentioned CMMI components are not satisfied.

This is where the GAP analysis is handy. You might be thinking about the current situation and the future state that you want your organization to reach, along with the task or tasks that need to be completed to close the gap.

While performing the gap analysis, a gap report (draft) is prepared for each process area. The draft report contains all the weakness within the organization. This draft is first presented to the management and key stakeholders. After their discussion, a final report will be prepared.

Figure 3-2 shows a sample gap report format with one process area: Project Planning (PP)

Sl No	Process Aea	Gaps	Elaboration	Recommendations					Implementation Recommendations	
				Process Change	Priority	Date(s)	Responsibility	Training	Implementation	
1	PP	Projects to estimate size, effort, schedule and cost based on life cycle adopted	Size : complexity in case of support and small enhancements, function point equivalents in case of bigger enhancements, assumptions, phase-wise effort and schedule distribution from CUT effort)	Prepare estimation template for Dev and Support Projects	2				All projects shall estimate size, effort and schedule using standard method (template)	

Figure 3-2. A sample gap report format

3.4.3 Plan and Close Identified/Reported Gaps

The next step is to analyze the gaps against the CMMI model, and then plan how to close the gaps within a timeline agreed upon by the management/key stakeholders. Note that this is also the time to plan or develop strategies for bringing the required cultural change to the organization. Cultural change is significant because, when closing the gaps, new paths and possibilities can emerge which we might have to adopt for the product and/or service delivery.

Based on the gaps reported, your organization can undertake the following steps:

- Determine the effort required to close all the reported gaps

- Assign individuals or teams to each gap to close

- Process gaps and update

- Update roles and responsibilities

- Target projects under CMMI implementation

- Update the organization's structure

- Assess the training needs for the teams

Based on the established plan, your organization can also do the following:

- Define the business goals and objectives

- Decide CMMI representation

- Decide on the maturity level to be achieved (e.g., Level 2 or Level 3)

- Decide on the timeline to achieve the targeted maturity level, business performance, and so on

- Track the plan/timeline for closing the gaps, as well as to achieve the targeted maturity level

---

■ **Tip**   Always be careful with the timeline you have selected to achieve your goal. Both relaxed and very aggressive timelines can affect quality of your implementation.

In terms of the CMMI implementation timeline, it is recommended that you be a little aggressive. One important point to note here is that you cannot skip any maturity level in between, which means you need to implement all the process areas belonging to a lower ML (maturity level). It is always recommended by the experts that you achieve ML3 before you move to ML4 and ML5.

Please remember that maturity level is not a rank, but rather the actual level of maturity for your organization. If we really want to benefit from CMMI Appraisal as an organization, then we need to perform at certain level with consistency. However, achieving a higher maturity level depends upon the organization's strength and willingness to do so.

■ **Caution**   If your process has a lot of gaps, then don't go to ML4 and ML5 directly because doing so could cause negative consequences and harm employee morale.

3.5 Summary

In this chapter, we learned about the steps to be taken to initiate the CMMI implementation, as well as points and questions we need to think about while initiating the implementation. We also learned how to identify and engage a CMMI partner, which groups and team formations would be needed, how process gap analysis is planned and conducted, and how to execute a plan for closing existing gaps.

CHAPTER 4

Creating, Updating, and Releasing a QMS

In this chapter, we will discuss creating, updating, and releasing a Quality Management System (QMS). We will also learn which teams the QMS is created for. For some, not only might *QMS* represent a new word, but its purpose might be unfamiliar, as well. If that's the case for you, it is recommended that you read about QMS from a CMMI appraisal perspective (see Chapter 6) because that will make it much easier to understand in the context of this chapter.

QMS is the combination of the policies, processes, templates, checklists, and guidelines which are used on a daily basis by employees or staff to create the software products/applications delivered.

4.1   Who Is QMS for?

To create the QMS for our employees and organization, we need to assess all the teams for which processes are needed. In fact, we have to create this for all the teams that are involved in delivering the software product or application.

A question could come to mind here: "Who will create the QMS?"

In earlier chapters, we discussed the SEPG and SQA/quality groups that will drive the process initiative cum compliance as a team in the organization.

Ownership of QMS resides with SEPG group to create, update, and release QMS to all the employees/staff.

Another question that might come to mind is this: "When does the SEPG group initiate the creation of the QMS?"

The answer is simple. It does so before we start building the software products or applications.

Also, the act of creating new processes or updating existing processes is initiated when an organization wants to implement CMMI practices. (This was discussed in Chapter 4 in the gap analysis exercise, where existing processes were reviewed against the CMMI model. After gap analysis, we come to know about the processes which are required to be created, both new ones and some existing ones that need to be updated or modified.)

Here's the most important point about QMS: all the processes must suit the need of your delivery and support teams, or else these processes won't be used and the expected results won't be achieved.

Hence, the SEPG team's main responsibility is to always identify the opportunities which could be analyzed to improve our processes.

Let's examine what goes into creating a QMS.

As stated in the model, we have to establish the organization's quality goals and objectives.

These quality goals and objectives set the organization's business objectives. For example, one goal is to provide on-time delivery of our software product/application to our clients.

Hence, as per the model, we need to define goals and objectives for the following teams:

© Mukund Chaudhary 2017
M. Chaudhary and A. Chopra, *CMMI for Development*, DOI 10.1007/978-1-4842-2529-5_4

- Software development

- Software maintenance

- Software engineering process group (SEPG),

- Quality Group

- Training Group

However, organizations can have goals and objectives for their other teams/groups which are supporting or involved in the software product/application delivery.

So, who initiates the goals/objectives exercise, and who are all the parties involved in creating it?

The SEPG group has to initiate this important exercise with senior management first, so it can identify the key goals that management/leadership team wants to set for the business, delivery, and support teams.

This exercise with the senior management is called a *goal question metric* (GQM). It helps to identify the business goals and objectives.

4.2   Interpreting a Goal Question Metric

If we have a goal for delivering on time or improving the delivery time, then we may need to ask the question, "What needs to be done or achieved to deliver on time?"

Once the way to achieve the goal has been identified, we need to link it with a metric to measure and assess goal accomplishment (see Figure 4-1).

Goals would be communicated by senior management for software delivery/ engineering teams, SEPG, and the quality and training groups.

Goal Question Metric

Goal Number	Goal /Process Improvement Objective Description	Question	Metric	Process Performance Parameter
Goal 1	On time delivery	Q1.1 Was the accuracy of estimating the actual value of project schedule?	Schedule Estimation Accuracy	Actual project duration/estimated project duration
		Q1.2. What was the accuracy of estimating the actual value of project effort?	Effort Estimation Accuracy	Actual Project Effort/ Estimated project effort
Goal 2	Increase defect containment.	Q2.What is the currently known effectiveness of each V&V activity to identify defects?	Defect Removal Efficiency	Number of pre release defects/number of pre release defects + number of post release defects

Figure 4-1. *A snapshot of a sample GQM*

Once the goals/business objectives are communicated, the SEPG team shall help in defining the associated metrics/measures to achieve them. The SEPG team shall hold a meeting with the delivery and functional team heads to discuss the required metrics/measures, their unit of measurement, data source, computation formula, frequency of data collection, and so on (see Figure 4-2).

Organization Quantitative Objectives												
Business Objectives	Measure	Target Range		Unit of Measure	Indicator Definition	Computation	Data Input	Data Source	Periodicity		Interpretation Guidelines		Tool For Analysis
		Min Value	Max Value						Collection	Analysis	Project	Organization	
To Deliver On Time	Schedule Variance	-10%	10%	Percentage	Extent to which number of days the delivery was varied from the planned delivery date (against planned and revised schedule)	Against planned schedule (Actual Duration – Planned Duration) * 100/ (Planned Duration) / Against revised schedule (Actual Duration – Revised Planned Duration) * 100/ (Revised Planned Duration) / Where Duration = End Date – Start Date / Calculate variation for every iteration / release / Revised Date : The last revision date and not the earlier revised dates	1. Planned start date for the release/ iteration 2. Actual start date for the release/ iteration 3. Planned end date for the release/ iteration 4. Actual end date for the release/ iteration	Schedule Tracker	Monthly /End of Phase / activity/ release	End of phase / release	1. The schedule variance trend should be improving (i.e. Schedule deviations moving towards zero) 2. The trend should be leading to achieve the set improvement goals	1. To meet the organizational goal for the year, if any 2. Half yearly trend to be positive	Line Graph with Trend

Figure 4-2. A snapshot of a delivery team (sample) business objective with metrics

■ **Note** In the Target Range column, Min Value and Max Value have to be derived from past projects' performance data in order to determine the Measure for Schedule Variance.

If performance data for past projects is not available or the organization has just started its operations, then the organization can analyze available industry standards/benchmarks for their identified measures.

If an organization cannot find suitable standards, then it can define or set its own target range for each metric/measure to start with. After a period of time based on the observed performance, Target Range (Min Value and Max Value) could be updated or improved.

Business objectives and associated metrics/measures may vary from organization to organization. Hence, each organization can define its objectives/measures based on its needs (see Figures 4-3, 4-4, and 4-5).

SEPG Quality Objectives													
Business Objectives	Measure	Targets		Unit of Measure	Indicator Definition	Computation	Data Input	Data Source	Periodicity		Interpretation Guidelines	Causal Analysis Trigger	Tool For Analysis
		Min	Max						Collection	Analysis	Project	Project	
Improve process through innovation and learning	Process Improvements Implemented	NA	NA	Number	1. Number of technology changes implemented 2. Number of process changes implemented 3. Number of audit preventive actions implemented 4. Number of process improvement activities (PI Goals) implemented 5. Number of project/ Services feedback analysis preventive actions implemented	None	Count of completed Technology Changes Count of Process improvement (PI Goals) action items Count of closed preventive actions Count of closed action items (causal analysis)	New Technology Implementation Plan Tracker	Monthly	Monthly	1. Trend of actions completed in time should be positive 2. The trend should be leading to achieve the set improvement goals, if any	1. Quarterly trend of actions closed on time should be positive	1. Trend not positive leading to achieve improvement goals, if any
Improve processes through innovation and learning	Effort spent on process improvement activities	NA	NA	Number	Effort spent on process improvement activity(Person Hours)	Number of hours spent towards process improvement activity	Number of hours spent towards process improvement activity	Timesheet/tool, Quality function status report	Monthly	Quarterly	1. Effort spent on process improvement activities trend should be increasing 2. The trend should be leading to achieve the set improvement	1. Trend not being positive 2. Trend not leading to achieve the set improvement goal	Line Graph with Trend

Figure 4-3. A snapshot of the SEPG team (sample) business objective with an associated Measure

83

SQA Quality Objectives											
		Targets		Unit of Measure					Periodicity	Interpretation Guidelines	Causal Analysis Trigger	
Business Objectives	Measure	Min	Max		Indicator Definition	Computation	Data Input	Data Source	Collection	Analysis	Project	Project	Tool For Analysis
Improve execution effectiveness	Audits conducted as per schedule	NA	NA	Percentage	Internal audits conducted as per schedule, as against the total number of internal audits scheduled	Audits conducted as per schedule / Total number of audits conducted * 100	Total number of audits conducted Audits conducted as per schedule	Internal Quality System Audit Report	End of audit	End of audit	1. Trend shall be leading to achievement of set target / goals	1. Trend not leading to achievement of set target / goals	Line Graph
Improve execution effectiveness	Closure of Non-conformance on time	NA	NA	Percentage	Audit non-conformances closed on time, as against the total number of audit non-conformances	Number of audit non-conformances closed on time / Total number of audit non-conformances * 100	Total number of audit non-conformances Number of audit non-conformances closed on time	Internal Quality System Audit Report	Quarterly	Quarterly	1. Trend shall be leading to achievement of set target / goals	1. Trend not leading to achievement of set target / goals	Line Graph

Figure 4-4. *A snapshot of the quality/SQA team (sample) business objective with an associated Measure*

Training Quality Objectives											
		Target	Unit of Measure					Periodicity	Interpretation Guidelines	Causal Analysis	
Business Objectives	Measure	Min		Indicator Definition	Computation	Data Input	Data Source	Collection	Analysis	Project	Project	Tool For Analysis
Improve execution effectiveness	Quality of training programs	90%	Percentage	Percentage of training programs achieving rating >= 3 (Out of 5)	(Number of programs achieving rating >= 3)* 100 / Total number of programs conducted	Feedback rating on training provided	Training Feedback form, Training Feedback Summary form, Training database	Monthly	Quarterly	1. The quality of training programs trend should be improving 2. The trend should be leading to achieve the set improvement goals if any	1. Trend not being positive 2. Trend not leading to achieve the set improvement goal	Line Graph
Improve Training Effectiveness	Training effectiveness rating	90%	Percentage	Training effectiveness rating to be computed for each course. A given course is designed for attaining a level of knowledge. On completion of training, employee is assessed to verify to have achieved targeted skill and knowledge level. Their % is computed out of the total participants.	(Number of employees assessed to have achieved targeted knowledge and skill level) * 100 / Total number of employees who have taken the course	1. Number of participants of the course who have achieved targeted knowledge and skill level 2. Total number of employees who have taken the course	Training Record, Record of work and development form	Quarterly	Quarterly	1. The training effectiveness rating trend should be improving 2. The trend should be leading to achieve the set improvement goals if any	1. Trend not being positive 2. Trend not leading to achieve the set improvement goal	Line Graph

Figure 4-5. *A snapshot of the training team (sample) business objective with an associated Measure*

By following the preceding sample snapshots of business objectives and measures, an organization (or its teams) can define its own relevant objectives and associated metrics/measures.

4.3   Creating Policies and Processes

We need to initiate the creation of policies and processes (e.g., procedures and SOPs). Once the GQM, business objectives, and metrics/measures exercise is done, the SEPG team will focus on the creation of policies and processes. (As pointed out in the earlier chapters, the SEPG and quality teams will drive the creation of QMS (i.e., its policies, processes, templates, checklists, guidelines, etc.—some organizations combined their SEPG and SQA teams).

As per the CMMI, the policies of each process are important. Hence, first policies shall be created, as these policies help organizations seek the required commitment from the employees/staff to follow the process approach in executing project/product delivery tasks (see Figure 4-6).

If an organization has planned for a CMMI level 3 implementation, then policies have to be created for all 18 process areas. If an organization has planned for a high maturity CMMI level 5 implementation, then policies have to be created for all 22 process areas.

SI No.	CMMi Process areas	QMS process name	Policy statement
1	Project Planning Project monitoring and control Integrated project management	Project Management Process	Each project owner must develop maintain and follow a written plan that defines project goals, processes, and resource estimates. The project plan must be updated through the life of the project to accurately reflect the current plan. Program manager must continuously track the progress of all projects against the project plans
2	Risk Management	Risk Management Process	Risks associated with each Information Technology project must be identified, analyzed, and prioritized. Identified risks must be controlled through the processes of project planning and monitoring. Risk identification and management must be integrated components of project management and risks must be continuously assessed and analyzed during the life of the project.

Figure 4-6. *A snapshot of (sample) policies, for reference purposes*

In the preceding snapshot, the following columns are covered:

- CMMI process areas, as per the CMMI model

- A QMS process name, which is given to the process that will be followed by the organization

Also, note that serial no. 1 includes three process areas in the "CMMI Process areas" column; however, the "QMS process name" column has only one process mentioned. This is because the project management process is defined by referring to the three process areas.

Hence, it is not necessary that we also create 18 (level 3) or 22 (level 5) process areas. We can group two or three CMMI process areas into one process.

Now let's look at the processes which we need to create as part of the QMS based on the CMMI model (see Table 4-1).

Table 4-1. *The QMS Processes to Be Created*

SI No.	CMMI Process areas as per model	QMS process name within organization	Remarks
1	Project Planning Project monitoring and control Integrated project management	Project Management Process	Three CMMI process areas can be grouped together into one QMS process (i.e., Project Management)
2	Risk Management	Risk Management Process	
3	Requirements Management	Requirements Process	Both Requirements Management and Development process areas could be grouped into one QMS process (i.e., Requirements Process)
4	Requirements Development	Requirements Process	
5	Technical Solution	Design Process	Here, one Technical Solution process area is covered in two different QMS processes
6	Technical Solution	Code & Unit Testing Process	
7	Product Integration	Build and Release Process	
8	Verification	Review Process	
9	Validation	Testing process	
10	Configuration Management	Configuration Management Process	
11	Measurement & Analysis	Measurement & Analysis Process	
12	Process & Product Quality Assurance	Quality Assurance Process	
13	Decision Analysis & Resolution	Decision Analysis & Resolution Process	
14	Organization Process Definition Organization Process Focus	Process Management Process	Two CMMI process areas can be grouped together into one QMS process (i.e., Process Management)
15	Organizational Training	Training Process	
16	Supplier Agreement Management	Supplier Process	

4.4   Creating Templates, Checklists, and Guidelines

For each QMS process, there will be associated templates, checklists, and guidelines which need to be created. Table 4-2 covers some sample items for a QMS implementation.

Until CMMI level 3 is achieved, the following QMS templates, checklists, and guidelines will be created. These might be sufficient to have from the implementation perspective, but each organization may create less or more of these items, based on its simple or complex work nature.

Table 4-2. *A Sample QMS for Level 3 Practices*

SI No.	QMS process name within organization	Template(s)	Checklist (s)	Guideline(s) if any
1	Project Management Process	1. Project Initiation Note 2. Project Kick Off 3. Integrated Project Plan 4. Estimation 5. Work Break Structure (excel) or Microsoft Project Plan (MPP) 6. Status Report 7. Minutes of Meeting 8. Action Log 9. Project Closure Report 10. Project Lessons Learned	1. IPP Review Checklist 2. Milestone Review Checklist 3. Project Closure Checklist	
2	Risk Management Process	1. Risk & Issue Log	1. Risk Identification Checklist	
3	Requirements Process	1. Requirements Understanding & Clarification 2. Business Requirement Specification 3. Software Requirement Specification 4. Requirement Traceability Matrix 5. Change Request Log/ Tracker 6. Change Request Form	1. Requirements Elicitation Checklist 2. Requirement Review Checklist	
4	Design Process	1. High Level Design 2. Low Level Design 3. Make Buy Reuse Analysis Report 4. User Manual	1. Design Review Checklist	
5	Code & Unit Testing Process	1. Unit Test Plan 2. Unit Test Case 3. Unit Test Report	1. Unit Test Plan Review Checklist 2. Code Review Checklist	Coding guidelines—.net, java, C, C++, PHP, and so on; an organization can create these based on its project work
6	Build and Release Process	1. Build Note 2. Release Note 3. Product Integration Plan	1. Build Review Checklist 2. Final Delivery Checklist	

(*continued*)

Table 4-2. (*continued*)

SI No.	QMS process name within organization	Template(s)	Checklist (s)	Guideline(s) if any
7	Review Process	1. Review Report To log the Review comments	1. Review Checklist To add the comments which must be verified during the reviews	
8	Testing process	1. Test Plan 2. Test Case 3. System Test Report 4. Defect Analysis	1. System Test Case Review Checklist 2. System Test Plan Review Checklist	
9	Configuration Management Process	1. Configuration Status Accounting	1. Configuration Audit Checklist	
10	Measurement & Analysis Process	1. Quality Objectives 2. Project Metrics Report 3. Department wise Metrics Report i.e. SEPG, SQA & Training		
11	Quality Assurance Process	1. Annual Quality Plan 2. Audit Plan 3. Audit Report 4. IQA Summary Report 5. List of Auditors 6. Process Compliance Report 7. SQA Monthly Summary Report 8. SQA Metrics Report		
12	Decision Analysis & Resolution Process	1. DAR Template		1. DAR Guidelines Provides guidance to perform DAR by using various methods
14	Process Management Process	1. SEPG Plan 2. SEPG status report 3. QMS Release Note 4. Pilot Plan 5. Deployment Plan 6. Process Improvement Request Form		1. Tailoring Guideline Provides guidance and informs staff at which phases tailoring is allowed

(*continued*)

Table 4-2. (*continued*)

SI No.	QMS process name within organization	Template(s)	Checklist (s)	Guideline(s) if any
15	Training Process	1. Annual Training Plan 2. Monthly Training Plan 3. Employee Skill Record 4. Training Request Form 5. Trainer Database 6. Trainer Evaluation Form 7. Attendance Sheet 8. Training Needs Analysis 9. Training Feedback Form 10. Training effectiveness and evaluation 11. Training Closure Form 12. Training Metrics		
16	Supplier Process	1. Vendor Selection Note: Remaining templates would be similar to those used for monitoring the projects; please refer to Sl No. 1	1. Vendor Selection Checklist	

For implementing CMMI level 4 and 5 practices following QMS- processes, templates, checklists and guidelines will be created (see Table 4-3).

Table 4-3. *A Sample QMS for Level 4 and 5 Practices*

SI No.	QMS process name within organization	Template(s)	Checklist (s)	Guideline(s)
1	Quantitative Project Management	1. Project Quality and process performance objective 2. Control Charts 3. Prediction Model	1.	1. Guideline to evaluate alternatives for selecting the subprocesses 2. Guideline to select measures and analytic techniques
2	Process Performance	1. Process capability baseline 2. Process performance model		1. Guideline to create process capability baseline 2. Guideline to create performance model 3. Definition of measures and their rationale for selection
3.		1. Pareto Analysis 2. Fish bone Analysis 3. 5 Why's		1. Guideline to perform RCA
4		1. List of improvements 2. Improvement proposal analysis 3. Improvement implementation plan and tracker 4. Improvement validation reports		1. Guideline to select the improvement areas and their rationale for selection

4.5   Updating QMS and Release QMS

In the preceding section, we learned, as part of the QMS, which processes, templates, checklists, and guidelines need to be created. In this section, we will learn about updating and releasing the QMS.

You might wonder whether it is important to know when the QMS gets updated, or why the need arises to update it.

4.5.1   The First Update

Before CMMI implementation, every organization always has some of the processes which it follows to deliver its software products or applications; however, when an organization decides to implement CMMI model/practices, the QMS gets updated in a full-grown manner.

4.5.2   The Second Update

Once the QMS is functional and processes, templates, checklists, and guidelines are in use by the staff/employees, there are always going to be improvement requests which will be reported by the staff for SEPG analysis. This is because it is only by using the processes that we can judge whether the processes created are useful and adding value. These improvements could be small or big in nature. For example, even a very small change required in one template or one checkpoint needs to be added in a checklist. In other words, it may lead to changes in current processes, templates, checklists, and guidelines, or it may be required to create the new ones.

After analyzing all of the received process improvement requests, the SEPG team will work on them and eventually update the QMS. It is an important exercise, and it may require a lot of effort by the SEPG team and other staff members who get the opportunity to work on the QMS update. As a result, the organization/staff receives the improved processes, templates, guidelines, and checklists.

4.6   Releasing the QMS

Once the work is done on updating the QMS, the time arrives to release the update version to the employees/staff.

The QMS release is done in a planned manner by the SEPG team, with the help of the SQA team. Some processes which are updated or created new get piloted before their release because it is important to know whether or not they will work. This prevents a lot of defect generation, so the defects are never passed into the system. This also saves lot of effort and rework in correcting such defects.

To communicate about the impending QMS release, the SEPG shall update one QMS release form. This form will contain information about what has changed from the previous version of QMS, as well as what has been added to the new version of the QMS. For example, the previous version of the requirement process was v1.0; after the update, v1.1 will be released. The same applies for templates, checklists, and guidelines.

The SEPG has to communicate to all the employees/staff about the QMS release, even if only a few members/staff had shared the process improvement request. This will ensure that everyone in the organization is aware of how to use and follow the new processes, templates, checklists, or guidelines.

4.7   Summary

In this chapter, we learned about creating, updating, and releasing a QMS. Along the way, we also learned what will become part of the QMS as per the CMMI model, as well as which departments the QMS is created for. Finally, we learned when the QMS gets updated and what goes into the QMS release.

CHAPTER 5

Implement QMS

In previous chapters, we have covered policies, processes, templates, guidelines, checklists, and other standards to be used for the various groups and departments based on CMMI levels. In this chapter, we will learn how to implement QMS for each department and group, as well as how to use different artifacts in our day-to-day activities. Let's start with how to plan a QMS training.

5.1   Plan QMS Training

We already have a QMS ready; now it's time to guide and train the employees/group on how to use it.

Once the QMS is released to everyone in the organization or the business unit teams, it becomes essential to provide process training to the delivery and support functions (i.e., to SEPG, QA, and training).

Hence, SEPG team has to plan process training with the help of the training team members. If your IT group or business unit targeted for CMMI implementation is big, then you should plan to implement the process training in multiple batches, as it would be difficult for everyone to attend the training on the same day. Hence, it also makes sense to deliver the process training in small batches.

In the process training, the trainer needs to explain to the teams how an employee can use and execute the process steps, including the associated artifacts they would need to create.

Note   The trainer for these process trainings should be the person from SEPG or the person who has written that particular process, as it will help the employees to understand it better.

5.2   Create and Update Project and Department Artifacts

Once the training is imparted to the delivery teams, the next step would be to convert the entire QMS templates into the usable project artifacts. All the project managers from different projects would have to start the documentation activities in their respective projects.

Let's look at which artifacts are required to be prepared by the project manager, the team members, and the SEPG/SQA/training functions.

The project manager documentation list includes the following:

- Integrated Project Plan

- Estimation

- Work Breakdown Structure (WBS)

- Risk & Issue Log

© Mukund Chaudhary 2017
M. Chaudhary and A. Chopra, *CMMI for Development*, DOI 10.1007/978-1-4842-2529-5_5

- Action Items Log
- Project Metrics
- Defects Analysis
- Decision Analysis & Resolution (DAR)

The engineering team needs to include the following documentation:

- Software Requirement Specification (SRS)
- SRS Review Comments/Log
- Design—High Level & Low Level
- High Level & Low Level design review comments/Log
- Unit Test Plan & Test Cases
- Unit Test Plan & Test Cases review comments/Log
- Unit Test Report/Results
- Integration Test Plan & Test Cases
- Integration Test Plan & Test Cases review comments/Log
- Integration Test Report/Results
- Build creation & Build Note
- System Test Plan & Test Cases
- System Test Plan & Test Cases review comments/Log
- System Test Report/Results
- Create release
- Release note

The SQA (Quality/Audit) team needs to include the following documentation:

- Quality cum audit plan
- Audit Reports
- Process compliance reports
- Quality cum SQA metrics

The training team needs to include the following documentation:

- Training Needs Analysis
- Annual Training Plan
- Training Calendar
- Training Attendance Records
- Training Feedback Records
- Training effectiveness records
- Training Metrics

The SEPG team needs to include the following documentation:

- SEPG Plan

- Process Improvement Tracker

- Process Improvement filled forms

- Process tailoring guidelines

- Process tailoring requests/records

- QMS release notes

- QMS Master list (for tracking of all the processes, templates, checklists, and guidelines)

- Knowledge repository (historical documents from the projects)

■ **Note** The preceding lists are not the complete, but it is advisable that you create all of the artifacts listed in them.

As a part of the project management plan, it is the responsibility of the project manager to keep all of the artifacts updated; the SEPG has to ensure that these are followed and institutionalized.

5.3   Conduct Implementation Reviews/Audits

Along with documentation exercise, the SEPG will have to plan and conduct the implementation reviews with the help of the quality/audit team. Implementation reviews will ensure that the documentation is compliant as per the CMMI model practices.

It is advisable to plan the implementation reviews during the creation of the documents; this helps the review quality team guide the documentation owners in an easy way. It also helps them to understand the process in an efficient manner.

5.3.1   Conduct Audits

After implementation reviews, the organization/SEPG team needs to plan internal audits to be compliant with the CMMI model. To conduct the internal process quality audits, the organization can opt to use its internal auditors/SMEs, or it can hire an external auditor cum consultant.

One must understand the meaning of the terms internal and external. The term *internal* indicates that the internal auditor can be any employee of the organization who has knowledge of the CMMI model, understands the project delivery, and can guide project team for implementation. Also, an auditor must have sufficient skills for metrics data calculation, as well as the ability to understand and audit the measurement activities in the project.

Audits will help in sharing the documentation gaps, and it will help the project/delivery teams to close the gaps in an easy and efficient manner.

■ **Note** The CMMI auditor must have taken the official CMMI Intro Training, so that he/she can have complete understanding of the CMMI model. He/she should also know how to implement the required process areas and Specific Practices.

5.3.2 Maintain Project Documentation

After implementation reviews and internal audits, the project/support functions have to maintain the created documentation in their respective areas. And once the spot check by the external consultant is planned, the created documentation can be verified.

5.4 Create and Update the Knowledge Repository

The CMMI model helps us to create a knowledge repository in the organization; it is the responsibility of the SEPG group to take the initiative for creating this repository, which is also referred to as the Process Asset Library (PAL) in the CMMI model. This repository will be available centrally to all in the organization, although they will have different access rights.

In the knowledge repository, we can have both product and process artifacts for reference purposes. The purpose of this repository is to provide help to the delivery and support functions, so they can use historical documents which can act as a guide cum help.

For example, a project manager during the project planning phase in a new project can refer to the historical project plan. This might include estimates which will help in providing the useful information to the team; by referring to these documents, the team can avoid any risks which might have occurred in the past projects.

Also, if a code repository is available, then the project manager and the delivery team can analyze and use some of the available reusable code, which will help them to reduce their work and to improve their overall delivery timelines.

A knowledge repository typically will include the following artifacts:

- Project Plan document

- Estimation records

- Past risks list

- Past issues list

- DAR records

- Reusable source code

- A lessons learned list based on past projects

- Defects list

■ **Note**   The SEPG team is responsible for updating the knowledge repository, but it is the responsibility of every member in the organization to contribute back to the repository.

5.5 Summary

In this chapter, we talked about the implementation of a QMS and how to train the employees/team to follow the new practices. We also discussed the project and support function artifacts that would be updated from time-to-time. This chapter also covered when to conduct the implementation reviews and internal quality audits within an organization, as well as the importance of this process. Finally, the chapter covered the need to maintain a knowledge repository and how to use it.

CHAPTER 6

■ ■ ■

Plan for CMMI Appraisal

In this chapter, we will cover how to plan and organize a CMMI appraisal for your group or organization, how to prepare and guide your teams for final CMMI appraisal, and how final appraisal activities are conducted. By the end of this chapter, we will have touched on most of the things which are required to plan for a successful CMMI Implementation. Specifically, this chapter will cover the following points:

- Identify the objective, constraints, and scope of an Appraisal
- Identify/develop an appraisal plan
- Prepare and train the team on appraisal methods
- Plan and prepare for appraisal conduct

Let's start with the first point of planning for a CMMI appraisal.

6.1   Identify the Objectives, Constraints, and Scope of an Appraisal

For most readers, this point is more like a generic practice. Whenever any project gets started, the first task is to analyze the requirements, and after that, to identify the objectives and scope.

6.1.1   Analyze the Requirements

For CMMI or any other appraisals, analyzing the requirements can be the most important process because it can be the foundation of success or failure for the complete appraisal. Most appraisal downfalls are due to a lack of requirements gathering.

From a CMMI perspective, the purpose is to understand the business needs of the organization for which the appraisal need to be conducted. The appraisal team leader of the lead appraiser (LA) will collect information and help the business head, unit head, or sometimes, the sponsor.

Various tools and techniques can be used for analyzing the requirements, such as interviewing the sponsor to get the needed information. A formal consultation is very important; sometimes, a series of meetings need to be conducted with the stakeholders for their consensus on the business needs, which can be done using a SCAMPI A appraisal.

© Mukund Chaudhary 2017
M. Chaudhary and A. Chopra, *CMMI for Development*, DOI 10.1007/978-1-4842-2529-5_6

6.1.2   Identify the Appraisal Objectives

With the series of meetings conducted, the business needs have been identified. In general, CMMI is requested when the organization or the business unit wants to accelerate its process improvement, which includes one or more of these parameters:

- Improving quality

- Reducing efforts and/or cost

- Decreasing time to market

There can be a variety of reasons for an organization to conduct a CMMI appraisal. For example, it can be driven by business objectives like the following:

- Documenting the benchmark that reflects business process improvements

- Identifying the potential risk areas of an organization which may impact the performance of an organization

- Supporting scientific decision making based on data and analytics

- Identifying the strength, weakness, opportunity and threat (SWOT) of the organization or business unit

As per the CMMI handbook, the appraisal team leader will ensure the following:

- The sponsor and relevant stakeholders are identified

- The business objectives have been documented (these will be provided by the sponsor)

- Whether the appraisal objectives have been aligned with the business objectives

- The appraisal usage mode has been identified (i.e., internal process improvement, supplier selection, or process monitoring)

■ **Note**   It is very important to schedule one meeting/discussion between the appraisal team leader and the CMMI sponsor (within the organization).

6.1.3   Identify Appraisal Constraints

The constraints can also be determined by scheduling the discussion between the lead appraiser and the sponsor and/or business head. The business/unit head must communicate whether there are any limitations which require negotiation with the lead appraiser.

Some constraints, like cost and schedules, can be identified at early stages of the appraisal, which are at a high level only. Examples of some basic constraints include the following:

- We need this Appraisal to be done in Q3 or Q2.

- You cannot use more than ten people on the team.

- Management review can be done only via a video conference, teleconference, or through similar technology.

6.1.4   Determining Appraisal Scope

The scope of the appraisal consists of the appraisal reference model (i.e., CMMI DEV, CMMI Services, or CMMI Acquisition) and the scope of the organization/unit that would be assessed during the appraisal.

The organization must ensure that the scope of the reference model is determined and documented early in the planning process. It can do so by using the staged representation or the continuous representation.

When we say organizational unit, we are referring to a subgroup within the organization for which appraisal activities will be carried out.

■ **Note**   An organization may include the whole organization or a business unit (it could be small or big) within the organization, or it may select only a few development projects for the CMMI implementation and appraisal/ratings.

As per the CMMI handbook, the following are the required practices for identifying the scope of the appraisal. The lead appraiser, along with the appraisal sponsor and/or the business/unit head, shall do the following:

- Identify the scope of reference model and representation that will be used for the appraisal

- Identify the organizational unit and scope to be assessed

- Identify team members who will participate in the appraisal

In the appraisal scope, we have to identify sample projects which could be assessed, as well as the support functions (i.e., SEPG, QA, and training). In the project scope, we must also include the organizational unit size (i.e., the total number of people currently working within the organizational unit and the total projects which are currently active).

As per the CMMI handbook, the sample projects and support functions have to showcase the following during the appraisal:

- *Primary projects*: Objective evidence for each process area under the scope of appraisal

- *Secondary projects*: Objective evidence for one or more process areas under the scope of appraisal

- *Support functions*: Objective evidence for practices under the scope of appraisal

6.2   Develop Appraisal Plan

Like any other plan, the appraisal plan is very important. It will act as a guide for the execution of appraisal activities. The lead appraiser will document the appraisal plan will share his/her review with the sponsor. A tool for developing the appraisal plan could be an appraisal plan template.

An appraisal plan may include the following appraisal planning activities:

- Tailoring method

- Resources required

- Cost and schedule

- Logistics

- Risks

- Appraisal plan commitment

Let's drill down in detail on each activity required for the development of an appraisal plan, beginning with the tailoring method.

6.2.1   The Tailoring Method

In concert with SCAMPI A, some of the tailoring which could be allowed is as follows:

- Depending upon the choices, there could be options within the required practices

- Parameters could be allowed to vary within the limits

- The SAM (Supplier Agreement Management) process area is optional, and it can be mentioned as out of scope for the organization or the business unit going for an appraisal

For SCAMPI A, the tailoring activities should be performed carefully because what should be tailored or made out of scope as per the model is very important for the business unit to be appraised. For example, consider a case where an organization wants the SAM process area to be out of scope for the appraisal as currently there is no outsourcing work, but the company's senior management has been in discussions to outsource some of its work to vendors in the near future (i.e., the SAM process area). If the CMMI team is not aware of this update from management, then there is a chance that the team will make the wrong tailoring selection. To avoid such scenarios, the CMMI team should be in constant touch with its senior management before making any decisions for the appraisal activity.

The CMMI guidelines expect the lead appraiser to do the following:

- Perform a review of each activity and select tailoring options accordingly

- Ensure that the tailoring decisions taken are appropriate to meet the appraisal objectives and constraints

- Ensure that the decisions made for making particular tailoring options are documented

---

■ **Note**   An organization must ensure that selected method tailorings and their implementation do not violate SCAMPI A Required Practices.

6.2.2   Identify Needed Resources

When conducting the appraisal, identify and estimate the resources required. Resource categories to keep in mind for the appraisal include human resources, infrastructure facilities, tools, and so on.

We have to ensure these resources are accounted for in advance because this will help the appraisal activities run more smoothly.

As per the CMMI guidelines, the lead appraiser will do the following:

- Ensure that the appraisal team members are identified by the business unit which needs to be appraised, as these appraisal team members need to participate in the final appraisal with the lead appraiser. These members should have sufficient experience in project management and engineering (i.e., SDLC)

- Ensure that the participants (i.e., functional area representatives (FAR)) from various project teams are identified by the business unit; FAR areas include requirements, design, coding and unit testing, and integration and testing

- Ensure that equipment and facilities have been arranged by the business unit

- Ensure that resource decisions are documented in the appraisal plan

---

■ **Note** If appraisal team members (ATMs) are not available for the SCAMPI A appraisal from within the organization, then, as per CMMI guidelines, the business unit is allowed to hire ATMs from outside the organization for the appraisal duration.

Also, during the appraisal planning, it's important to identify the projects to be appraised, along with names of the people who are going to participate as team members in the appraisal.

You also need to identify the seating capacity and environment of the rooms which will be used by the teams for conducting the appraisal activities. Please be aware that resource planning is not limited to the personnel only; it is also includes a projector, laptop, or video-conferencing equipment (for any teams or senior members who are not present when the business unit is to be appraised).

6.2.3   Determine the Cost and Schedule

After estimating the resource requirements, you need to estimate the cost and schedule; as per the CMMI guidelines, there are required practices for estimating the cost and schedule. The lead appraiser will do the following:

- Estimate key appraisal events for the required duration in order to form a detailed schedule

- Estimates the effort of participating members in the appraisal

- Estimates the cost for using the business unit facilities and equipment, as appropriate

- Estimate the cost for any travel, lodging, and meals, as required at the time of appraisal

- Document the detailed appraisal plan

6.2.4   Manage Logistics

The next step is to manage the logistical plan which must take in the details and should be documented. The team leader must document logistical schedule and dependencies if any. They must maintain the communication channel for providing status and assign responsibilities to track logistical issues.

To make the logistical planning more effective, you must plan for the following details:

- Hotels or guest houses for the members and lead appraiser, if travel is required to perform the appraisal at different locations or even outside the country

- Any workstation support

- The arrangement of food and beverages

- Good Internet connections and other accessible equipment that might be required during the appraisal

6.2.5   Document and Manage Risk

As with any other project risks, it is very important to plan and manage risks proactively for the CMMI appraisal. The lead appraiser will document the identified risks and associated mitigation plans. The lead appraiser will also communicate these risks and their associated mitigation plans to the CMMI sponsor, CMMI team leader, and the ATMs.

6.2.5.1   Obtain Commitments to the Appraisal Plan

This is the final step for developing an appraisal plan, where the formal commitment is obtained from the sponsor. The appraisal plan constitutes an agreement between sponsor and the lead appraiser.

The lead appraiser will do the following:

- Ensure that the appraisal plan is reviewed with the sponsor and that the sponsor's approval is secured

- Ensure that the appraisal plan is also reviewed with the relevant stakeholders for their review and acceptance

The lead appraiser and the sponsor have to sign the appraisal plan to secure the commitment towards the plan.

6.3   Prepare and Train the Team on Appraisal Methods

Once the appraisal plan is prepared and the commitment is obtained from the sponsor, it's time to ensure that an experienced and qualified team is ready to execute the appraisal process.

Approximately one month before the scheduled appraisal date, the lead appraiser will conduct the mandatory four day training session for the ATMs. Of the four total days, the CMMI intro session will be conducted for the first three days; and on the last day, the ATMs will be taught how to conduct the appraisal. This will help the ATMs to be clear on the concepts of CMMI, so that they will be ready to help the lead appraiser.

Every lead appraiser's teaching style is different; hence, ATM members can undergo a somewhat different appraisal experience if they get the chance to participate in more than one appraisal. However, if the lead appraiser is the same during the second CMMI appraisal, then the ATMs will have to wait for a new lead appraiser.

■ **Note** For some ATM members, it could be their second CMMI appraisal; in such a scenario, they don't need to attend the CMMI intro training again; instead, they need to attend only the one day training on how to conduct the appraisal, as attendance on this day is mandated by the CMMI Institute. There is one catch here, however; this scenario won't work if the version of CMMI model has changed since the last time that ATM member underwent the intro training.

6.4   Plan and Prepare for Appraisal Conduct

Here, the motive is to ensure readiness for conducting the appraisal. This readiness includes the availability of filled PIIDs which show the mapping of the CMMI model practices against the objective evidence from projects and support functions, as well as the availability of appraisal team members, updated risk status, and the associated mitigation plans.

Upon assessment, the sponsor and the lead appraiser will decide whether the appraisal plan will be executed as defined or need to be re-planned. They will also have to decide whether any corrective actions need to be taken against the plan to ensure that the plan is successfully achieved.

The lead appraiser will perform the following steps to check the readiness of the appraisal:

- Check the availability of objective evidence for each practice in the process area, as per the defined appraisal scope

- Ascertain the readiness of ATMs to conduct the appraisal

- Determine the availability and readiness of all the logistics (i.e., the infrastructure facilities, equipment, etc.)

- Review the status of appraisal risks and their impact

■ **Note** The readiness review can be assessed on-site, off-site, by video- or teleconference, or in a combined manner.

There will always be more than one readiness review, as there could be leftover gaps which the teams will need to work on and close.

6.5   Conduct the Final Appraisal

On the first day of the final appraisal, the opening meeting will be held in which the lead appraiser will present the appraisal plan to all the teams and the sponsor. Also, the lead appraiser will cover how the appraisal plan will be executed and the activities which are planned each day (i.e., documents review, interviews with different teams, etc.).

After the opening meeting, the lead appraiser will review the documents with the appraisal team members. Once this exercise is finished, the interview sessions will start the next day; usually, these sessions start with the project management interview, followed by the project team members, including the SEPG, QA, training, and management members (i.e., it could include the program manager).

Once all the interviews are finished, the lead appraiser will, along with the appraisal team members, consolidate the findings and assess whether there are any weakness/improvement points against any practice.

During this exercise, if there are any queries to be asked of a project manager or any other team member who has already been interviewed, then that person can be called back to the interview room for clarification. For example, during the interview session, a project manager might communicate that status reports are being shared with the program manager, but the objective evidence provided to the lead appraiser and appraisal members does not support this assertion. In this scenario, the project manager would be called again to show some evidences that the status reports have been communicated to the management. If evidence is available, then no weakness would be reported; however, there is a possibility that the improvement suggestion could be noted.

After all the evidence collection, interview sessions, and clarifications, the lead appraiser and appraisal team members will start rating each process area, specific goals, and/or generic goals.

If all the specific and generic goals are fully or largely implemented and satisfied, then only the overall organizational unit would be rated as satisfied. Once all the process areas have been rated, then the next step would be to prepare the findings presentation. All appraisal members will prepare their findings/slides, and these will be reviewed with the lead appraiser.

Once the slides are reviewed, they will be merged together to form the preliminary findings. These findings will be presented first to all the team members who were interviewed, so as to ensure that any finding which is noted is not incorrect.

After the preliminary findings session on the last day, the final findings presentation is done for all of the organizational unit and team members who participated. The findings are comprised of both strengths and weaknesses. Strengths document things we have to carry forward in the future, and weaknesses document areas we need to look at.

When all the findings are presented, the final slide will tell you the result, whether you are successfully appraised for CMMI Level 3 or CMMI Level 5, as per the appraisal scope.

6.6 Summary

In this chapter, we covered planning for identifying the scope, constraints, and objectives of the appraisal. We have also covered how to develop the appraisal plan, and clarified the roles and responsibilities of the appraisal team leader and the lead appraiser. This chapter also discussed how to prepare and plan for the appraisal.

CHAPTER 7

■ ■ ■

Focus on Continual Improvement

After the CMMI appraisal, our focus should not deviate from continual improvement. In this chapter, therefore, we will focus on how to achieve this principle. If the focus deviates from this, then the whole purpose of the CMMI implementation will be lost. Let's begin by breaking down what the term continual improvement means.

7.1 Continual Improvement

In a CMMI context, the continual improvement objective is to keep enhancing the QMS, including the processes, templates, guidelines, and checklists. A big part of this is identifying areas where we can improve.

7.2 Identify Improvement Areas

After the appraisal, our first task is to analyze the improvement areas list from the appraisal report. We also want to analyze other improvement areas identified and noted by the SEPG team.

Every improvement area needs to be analyzed for its potential benefit versus the effort required to implement it, as this will help us to strengthen the QMS. In Chapter 6, we covered how anyone can contribute ideas to improve it. Whenever anyone on the team identifies an area for process improvement, that person can raise the process improvement request to SEPG team (see Figure 7-1).

© Mukund Chaudhary 2017

M. Chaudhary and A. Chopra, *CMMI for Development*, DOI 10.1007/978-1-4842-2529-5_7

1   Process Change/Improvement details:

PI Feedback Number:				
The Following shall be filled by the Requestor				
Process Improvement / Change / New Technology Use Proposed:				
Reason For Change:				
Identified by:		Function:		
Recorded by:		Date:		
Impact Analysis:				

Sl No.	Affected Processes	Sl No.	Affected Process Documents / Tools/ Techniques	
1		1		
2		2		
3		3		
4		4		
5		5		
6		6		

<To be filled by SEPG>

SEPG Head/Process Owner:		Date:	

Process Improvement / Change Proposal Evaluation:

Sl No.	Parameters	Y/N/ NA	Remarks
1			
2			
3			
4			

(In case of conflict , item 1 shall prevail)

Decision by SEPG:
<Accepted / Rejected / Deferred >

Priority Assigned :

Change Type:

Figure 7-1. *The sample process improvement form*

The next step is to prepare the improvements for following teams:

- Project Delivery Team

- SEPG and QA

- Training

But as an organization, if there are other support departments (e.g., HR and Admin) that provide services to the preceding teams, then it makes sense for the organization to focus on improving the process for these teams, as well. This is because these other teams can also directly or indirectly impact the delivery of the project team for any xyz reasons.

Process improvement is a collective responsibility of the different teams within an organization, and the software process improvement group (SEPG) is responsible for implementing the process improvement.

▨ **Note**   It is not mandatory for the SEPG team to implement the request raised; the team can accept or reject the request, based on its own analysis.

7.3   Prioritize Improvement Areas

Once the improvement areas are identified or consolidated, the next important thing task is to prioritize the sequence of improvement areas in terms of which improvements will be implemented.

The SEPG team has to prioritize the improvements based on the implementation benefits proposed by the improvement.

Also, the SEPG team needs to ensure that the improvement list is reviewed and approved by senior management. During the review, senior management can also set the priority for various improvements, according to which requests it feels should be implemented first.

7.4   Prepare an Action Plan

Once the improvement areas are prioritized, the next step is to prepare the action plan for each improvement.

The action plan should capture the following information:

- An improvement description

- An improvement category (e.g., major or minor)

- How QMS artifacts are impacted (i.e., which processes, templates, checklists, and/or guidelines need to be updated or modified?)

- The training to be imparted or conducted

In the action plan, you should have a category for training and indicate "Yes" if training is required for the staff members based on the improvement. For example, if a new process is added into the QMS, then it is essential that staff members be trained on the new process or the modified/updated process.

If the improvement is minor, requiring only a small modification/update to the template and no training, then you need to indicate that no training is required.

You need to assign the improvement to a staff member. The assignment should include the following information:

- A target date of completion: The date by which the improvement implementation will be completed)

- The total effort planned (hours): Estimates the total hours required for the implementation

- Progress Update: The current phase of the update's progress

A progress update section might look like the following:

- Date: April 27, 2016
  Update: Process modification work is complete; template update is in progress
- Date: April 23, 2016
  Update: Work has been initiated on the process modification

Capturing the update in this manner will help in determining and assessing the progress of the update. For example, it can help you determine whether a given implementation can be completed by the mentioned target date.

The progress update can also mention whether there is any delay or issue due to xyz reason. For example, if any input/information or discussion is pending or stakeholders are not available, then such points should be captured:

- *Current Status*: States might include Open, In-Progress, On-Hold, Deferred, ImplementationComplete, or Closed

- *Implementation Review Period*: Mention the timeline or the number of days for which improvement will be monitored after the implementation to gauge its effectiveness

- *Implementation Review Status*: States might include Status-Satisfactory and Not-satisfactory (if the implementation isn't satisfactory, then it needs to be reviewed again)

- *Actual Completion Date*: Indicate the date on which implementation was completed

- *Actual Effort Spent (Hours)*: Indicate the total hours spent for implementing the improvement

---

■ **Note**   In scenarios where the status is put on hold, the target completion date needs to be extended or replanned.

7.5   Review and Monitor

Once the improvement is implemented, the next step is to review and monitor the affected areas (i.e., the projects or support departments affected by the implementation).

This step is important because we have to assess whether the improvement implementation is effective, including whether staff members are able to adapt to the improvement.

To determine the implementation's effectiveness, we need to define the parameters which might help in assessing the effectiveness level. If the result is found to be not satisfactory based on those defined parameters, then we have to analyze and identify the factors that caused the implementation to be ineffective.

For example, it might be that a few teams were not trained well in the new process. Consequently, the desired result could not be achieved. Or, it might be that the new defined process is not adding value, or its process execution time has increased. Or, perhaps not all teams are able to use the new/updated process; hence, a separate new process needs to be created for these teams.

Here, we need to re-create the action plan for the steps we need to implement again (in a second implementation cycle). The goal is increase the effectiveness of the planned improvement. Once the second implementation cycle is complete, it's time for the second round of the review and monitor cycle. We have to restart and reassess the effectiveness of this new change based on the defined parameters.

If the results are found to be satisfactory, then we can update the improvement implementation status as complete/closed.

7.6   Summary

In this chapter, we learned how to focus on continual improvement (i.e., the implementation of improvements which are reported through the appraisal report by lead appraiser or identified internally by the SEPG team by various means). We also learned how to implement these improvements, what steps are required to do so, and how to assess whether the implemented improvements are effective or satisfactory.

7.7   References

This book was created by taking some reference material directly from the CMMI model and augmenting that based on the experience of the authors. At this juncture, we believe we have covered the most of required things to plan for an appraisal, so we are closing our guide for CMMI implementation. We would like to thank you, the reader, for taking this journey with us, but also to remind you that nothing is perfect in this universe, not even the authors!

We hope you had a great learning experience!

Index

© Mukund Chaudhary 2017
M. Chaudhary and A. Chopra, *CMMI for Development*, DOI 10.1007/978-1-4842-2529-5

Get the eBook for only $4.99!

Why limit yourself?

Now you can take the weightless companion with you wherever you go and access your content on your PC, phone, tablet, or reader.

Since you've purchased this print book, we are happy to offer you the eBook for just $4.99.

Convenient and fully searchable, the PDF version enables you to easily find and copy code—or perform examples by quickly toggling between instructions and applications.

To learn more, go to http://www.apress.com/us/shop/companion or contact support@apress.com.

Printed in the United States
By Bookmasters